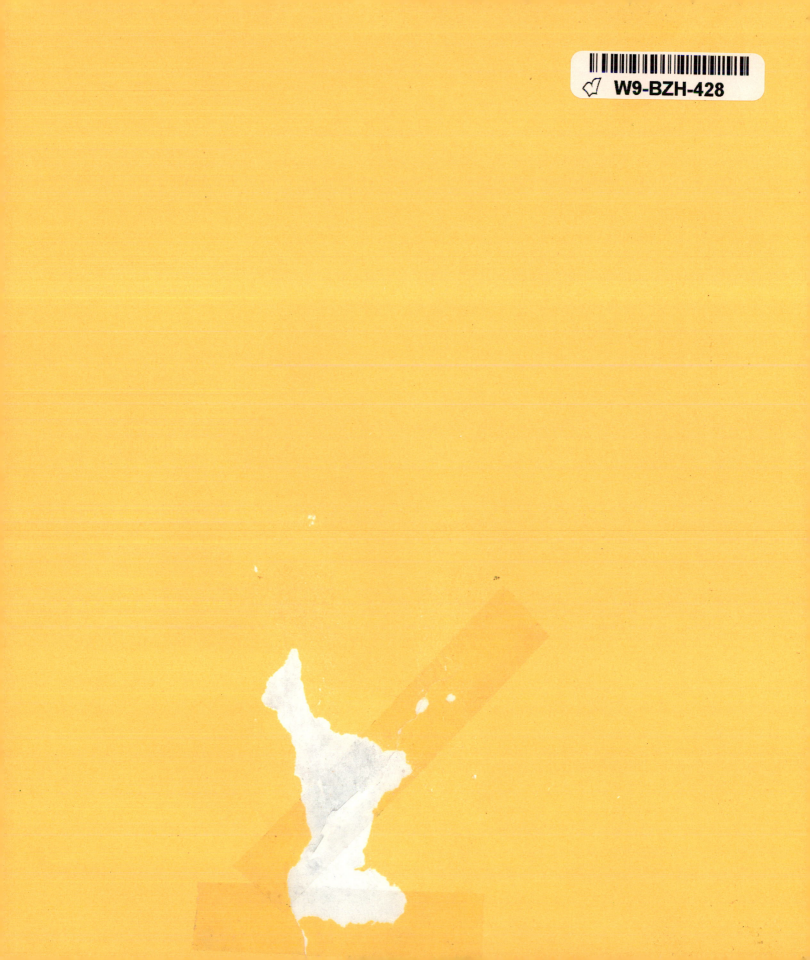

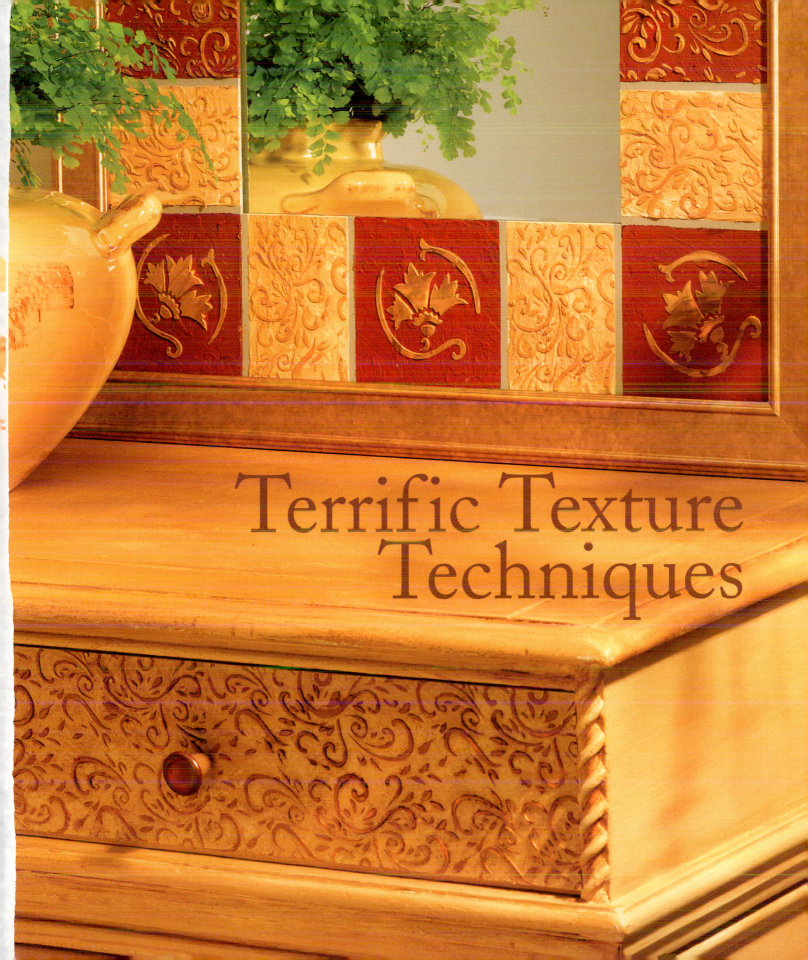

Terrific Texture Techniques

Terrific Texture Techniques

Decorating with Dimensional Finishes

By **Tiffany Windsor**

Delta Technical Coatings

Sterling Publishing Co., Inc. New York
A Sterling/Chapelle Book

Chapelle, Ltd., Inc., P.O. Box 9252, Ogden, UT 84409
(801) 621-2777 • (801) 621-2788 Fax
e-mail: chapelle@chapelleltd.com
Web site: www.chapelleltd.com

A Red Lips 4 Courage book
Red Lips 4 Courage Communications, Inc.:
Eileen Cannon Paulin, Catherine Risling,
Rebecca Ittner, Jayne Cosh
8502 E. Chapman Ave., 303
Orange, CA 92869
Web site: www.redlips4courage.com

Library of Congress Cataloging-in-Publication Data available

10 9 8 7 6 5 4 3 2 1

Published by Sterling Publishing Co., Inc.
387 Park Ave. South, New York, NY 10016
©2005 Delta Technical Coatings
Distributed in Canada by Sterling Publishing
c/o Canadian Manda Group, 165 Dufferin St.
Toronto, Ontario, Canada M6K 3H6
Distributed in Great Britain by Chrysalis Books Group
PLC, The Chrysalis Building,
Bramley Road, London W10 6SP, England
Distributed in Australia by Capricorn Link
(Australia) Pty. Ltd.
P.O. Box 704, Windsor, NSW 2756, Australia
Printed and Bound in China
All Rights Reserved

Sterling ISBN 1-4027-2144-7

FOREWORD

The Magic of Texture

Texture. Just the word *texture* conjures up different images for each of us. Texture surrounds us. Everywhere you look, you see and feel texture. You need only step outside into nature to see the inspiration that complements our everyday lives reflected in the fabrics in our clothing and home furnishings, carpets, wall coverings—even the seemingly smooth surfaces in architecture become textured and dimensional as you step back and gaze upon a downtown skyline.

With the introduction of new dimensional paint products, you don't need to be an artist to add texture to your own surroundings. For many years, only highly skilled artisans dared to venture into tinting various pastes and applying tinted textures to walls and home décor. Now, with pre-mixed dimensional paints, anyone can achieve beautiful dimensional textured effects. If you consider yourself in the novice category of "I've never tried anything like this before," then the ease of using stencils to apply textured designs will be very appealing. If you are more experienced, you will enjoy experimenting and layering with the various textured techniques shared in this book.

As a lifetime crafter and artist, I have enjoyed creative expression and the finished results. I have found in working with Delta's Texture Magic Dimensional Paint I can always achieve satisfactory results. I have put this dimensional paint to the test in many workshops and classes. It is so satisfying when first-time students lift their stencils to reveal their creative textured handiwork, declaring, "I can do this!"

As you will learn, in working with Texture Magic, there are no mistakes. If you don't like your first attempt, simply scrape off the dimensional paint and start over. From one-color applications to marbling, embedding, and faux-finish effects—whether you are creating beautiful gifts or enhancing your home décor—you will find creating with texture fast, fun, and achievable. Enjoy!

Tiffany Windsor

Tiffany Windsor

TABLE OF CONTENTS

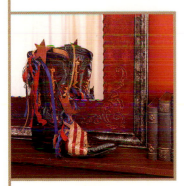

In a time when we are inundated with news reports and we are contactable virtually anywhere and at any time, the need to find breathing space has been elevated to a new level. At the heart of this is the desire to focus on our well being and to make sure our home is our haven. While we each have different lifestyles and design preferences, we can all relate to at least one of these styles. Projects can be adapted to a particular color palette or theme simply by changing paint colors or stencil designs. Which best describes you?

Nurture My Soul

The need to take care of ourselves has led to the simple joys in life—permission to take sips of serenity that replenish our souls throughout the day and help us cope with the stresses of our world. The Nurture My Soul color palette represents the natural elements of earth, wind, water, and fire with a strong focus on spirituality, Zen, relaxation, and cool, calming colors that evoke peace and serenity.

Global Mosaic

With wider world awareness, the elements, colors, and textures from other nations have made an impact on our design and décor. We frequently mix touches of other cultures into our lives and are richer for it. The Global Mosaic color palette tends to be more rich and earthy, with a few vibrant hues thrown in for visual contrast.

Fabulously Feminine

Today's woman has many strengths and styles. She is a determined being with an empowered softness. A celebration of all that is womanly and pretty can be expressed in variations that are soft and romantic. The Fabulously Feminine color palette varies from subtle to rich, and takes its inspiration from the current influences of romance, goddess, family, nurturing, bohemian, and flirty girls.

American Expressions

From American cottage to rustic cabin, our patriotic heritage has evolved from the obvious to the implied. The American Expressions color palette expresses an easy elegance with a touch of traditional and formal mixed in, along with an increase in natural materials such as fine woods. Hues that speak to this theme are a muted mixture of classics—cream and denim, adobe red, and foliage green.

Reflections

Our love affair with the past—the colors, textures, and styles—continues and many things retro or vintage reappear with a twist. The Reflections color palette reflects the eras of times gone by, including 1940s Hollywood Glamour, '50s ideas, '60s simplicity, and the shapes and patterns of the '70s.

Supplies

Dimensional paint: Special effects paint used to achieve dimensional stencil and faux-finish looks (A, B).

Foam brushes and small paint rollers: For applying basecoat acrylic colors and over paint for worn stenciled effect.

Lint-free soft cloths: For use when wiping antiquing applications.

Painter's tape: Also known as low-tack masking tape. Use to create straight-line applications or to mask off areas of stencil to keep colors separate. To create clean dimensional paint lines, always press tape firmly to surface prior to applying dimensional paint.

Palette: Apply paints onto palette, paper, paper plate, or waxed paper for easy mixing.

Paper towels: For drying stencils, tools, and hands.

Plastic zip-top bags: Use to store excess dimensional paint for use later.

Sandpaper: Sanding dimensional paint after it has dried gives worn or aged look. Use coarse sandpaper for quickest results.

Scissors: For trimming stencils to fit work surface.

Stencils: Thick or thin pre-cut plastic or brass designs.

Sticky notes: An easy tool for masking areas of stencils where you do not want to apply dimensional paint.

Tape: Apply low-tack masking tape to surface. Press edges firmly to surface.

Varnish: Use either spray-on or brush-on matte varnish.

Waxed paper: Use to clean and store stencils until next use; also excellent for protecting your work surfaces.

Wet wipes: For cleaning stencils, tools, and hands.

Glossary of Terms

Background stencils: Pre-cut designs in a small repeat pattern.

Basecoat: Apply 1, 2, or 3 coats of acrylic paint with soft bristle brush or foam roller; let dry completely between coats and after final coat.

Clean stencil: Place stencil on palette or waxed paper. Use spreader to scrape excess dimensional paint from stencil. If you plan to immediately reuse leftover paint, place it back onto palette. For future use, store excess in zip-top bag. Whenever possible, scrape one color at a time from stencil to re-use color. Leaving stencil on waxed paper, clean with wet wipe on front. Move stencil to clean waxed paper and continue to clean with wet wipes until all dimensional paint is removed. Before re-using stencil, be certain it is dry and test for stickiness of remaining spray adhesive.

Comb: Firmly drag comb through dimensional paint for desired effect.

Dry brush: Dip paintbrush into acrylic paint. Brush onto paper towel to remove nearly all paint from brush. Lightly brush over surface.

Embed: Press objects into wet dimensional paint.

Prepare stencil: Apply spray adhesive to back side of stencil according to label instructions (C). Let adhesive set for several minutes before applying to work surface.

Spread: The use of wide, flat, or pointed spreader to apply dimensional paint (D). Size and shape of spreader depends on application needs.

Preparing the Surface

Glass: Wash and dry surface.

Metal: Wipe clean and apply metal primer to metal and tin surfaces.

Papier Mâché: Apply dimensional paint to unfinished or painted papier mâché boxes.

Plastic: Wash and dry surface.

Wax: Wipe surface of wax with rubbing alcohol; let dry before beginning stencil process.

Wood: Sand and seal all wood surfaces.

Dimensional Paint

Textured dimensional paint is available in a variety of colors. The drying time of dimensional paint varies based on local conditions and thickness applied. In a 72º (22º C) non-humid room, a thin layer will dry to the touch in 20 to 30 minutes. A thick application will skin over in about 30 minutes but will take several hours to dry completely. On a cold day, have the room warmed to at least 72º (22º C). Use plastic zip-top bags to store excess dimensional paint scraped from your surface or the stencil during clean up.

Spreading the Paint

If you have ever frosted a cake or made a peanut butter sandwich, you can apply dimensional paint. Selecting the right spreader will make texture application easier. The wide spreader can be used for applying texture to larger areas and one-color applications over stencils. The flat spreader (A) is for spreading texture over stencils and for adding texture and pattern into the dimensional paint. The pointed palette knife is for spreading texture over small areas where color detail is important. The double-ended detailing tool can be used as a writing tool to create line details (B).

When spreading dimensional paint, you have several options for texture and thickness depending on your creative desires. The dimensional paint can be spread thin or thick, smooth or textured. For lots of texture and dimension, use a thicker application. Take some time and play with the dimensional paint and spreaders to develop your personal favorite techniques. If you apply the dimensional paint onto a palette or waxed paper, you can scrape it off and apply it over and over again while you test various applications for spreading the paint. Keep in mind that the dimensional paint will start to thicken and dry after approximately 30 minutes.

Stenciling

Dimensional paint works well with pre-cut stencils (C). Prepare the stencil by spraying the back side with repositionable stencil adhesive. Always follow label directions and spray stencils in properly ventilated area. The spray adhesive will help keep the stencil firmly attached to the surface so the dimensional paint won't slip or seep under the stencil. You may be able to reuse the stencil two or three times before needing to reapply stencil adhesive. Be sure to check stencil after each use and cleaning to see if adhesive needs to be reapplied.

When positioning stencil on surface, carefully but firmly, press and smooth down all edges of the stencil with fingers. Dimensional paint may be spread over stencils in a thin, thick, smooth, or textured application. Once you have spread dimensional paint over the stencil in desired application, carefully lift stencil (D)

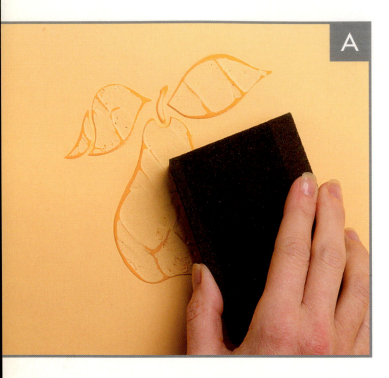

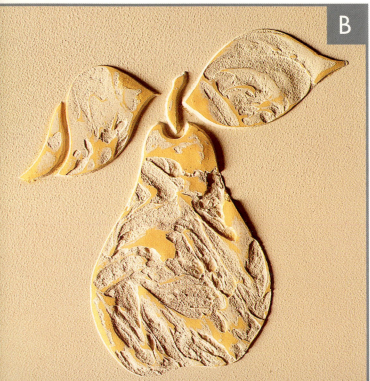

straight up. Depending on the thickness of your application, you may find some over-exaggerated peaks in the dimensional paint that can be gently removed with the double-ended detailing tool. Once the dimensional paint has dried, you may also remove these peaks by gently sanding the dried dimensional paint.

When stenciling a large, repeat design surface, trim the end(s) of the stencil so it does not overlap on the wet dimensional paint. Multiples of the same stencil can be used to stencil larger areas at one time without having to clean and reapply one stencil over and over.

When applying dimensional paint to the stencil, squeeze out paint directly from its tube onto project surface or a palette, then pick up with the spreader and apply onto stencil.

Removing dimensional paint from a stencil is easy. After lifting stencil from the work surface, place it on a palette or waxed paper. Using spreader, scrape excess dimensional paint from stencil. If you are going to immediately reuse the leftover paint, place it back onto the paper. If you would like to save the paint for future use, store excess in zip-top bag. Whenever possible, scrape one color at a time from stencil so that you may re-use that color. If dimensional paint has been mixed on the stencil (such as in highlighting or marbling applications), save excess in zip-top bag to be used in projects that will be over painted with acrylic paint.

Once you have scraped the excess paint from the stencil, clean stencil with wet wipe on front. Move stencil to clean waxed paper and continue to wipe until all dimensional paint is removed. Before reusing the stencil, be certain it is dry and check remaining spray adhesive to determine if adhesive needs to be re-applied. Sticky stencils may be stored on waxed paper.

The worn stenciling effect works well for styles including country, shabby and chic, and retro. This stenciling technique works in reverse color in that you first apply the dimensional paint in the color you want to show through in the end. After the stenciled design is dry, paint the entire project with acrylic paint. When dried, sand the edges of the stenciled areas with coarse sandpaper to reveal the colored dimensional paint (A). This technique looks fabulous on walls—think fruit for a country kitchen (B), fleur-de-lis for an elegant dining room, alphabet letters for a child's room, and flowers and leaves for a garden retreat.

Stamping

You can create beautiful effects by utilizing foam stamps with dimensional paint (C). Foam stamps create the best designs because of their broad surfaced designs. Depending on your desired finished effect, spread a thin or thick, smooth or textured layer of dimensional paint. Let paint set for approximately 10 minutes. Dip foam stamp into water, gently shake off excess, press stamp into dimensional paint (D), and lift. If you are not satisfied with the image, use spreader to re-spread dimensional paint and re-stamp. Once dimensional paint has dried, sand with coarse sandpaper to give image an aged effect. After stamping, clean foam stamp with a wet wipe immediately and use detailing tool to remove all dimensional paint from the stamp.

Other impressions can be made into dimensional paint including silk or real leaves with deep veins, burlap, textured fabrics, laces and trims, chicken wire, and a window screen. Look for interesting found objects that can be stamped into your dimensional paint projects.

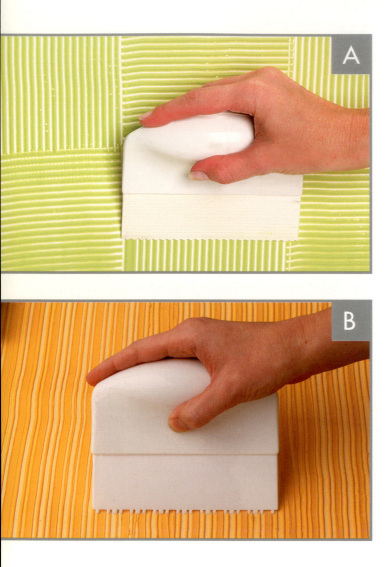

Combing

For dimensional looks with a graphic style, comb interesting patterns into dimensional paint. Kitchen tools work well for creating texture designs. Forks, knives, spoons, and other cooking gadgets can be used to draw patterns into dimensional paint. There are also combs designed specifically for use with dimensional paint and include patterns such as ridged, ticking, square tooth, and wave.

The key to successful combing is to first apply a smooth, thin layer of dimensional paint onto your surface. Next, firmly drag the comb through the paint. If you are not happy with the results, simply re-spread the paint onto the surface and start again. Many combed applications are combined with the taping of edges to create clean, straight lines. If using tape, for best results, be certain to press the edges firmly to the project surface.

Also, be sure to work in an area that does not touch any portion of wet stenciling. Once you have achieved the desired look in a particular area, remove the tape and let dry thoroughly before continuing combing technique in an adjacent area.

The key to success in this technique is a thin application of dimensional paint and short strokes of patterning. If you comb a larger or longer section, the dimensional paint tends to catch back into the comb, resulting in uneven patterning. Practice on waxed paper to determine your favorite designs.

Combs are available in a variety of styles. By simply mixing your strokes you can create a plaid pattern (A) or a pin stripe design (B).

Embedding

A fun and creative technique is embedding found objects into dimensional paint (C). This technique is easier and quicker than traditional mosaic because the dimensional paint acts as its own grout. Glass beads, wood, metal, mosaic tiles, alphabet lettering… just about anything can be pressed into dimensional paint.

Before you begin any project, be sure to clean your surface thoroughly. Vases should be washed with soap and water, rinsed thoroughly then allowed to dry. All other surfaces should be wiped with a soft cloth to remove any dust or particles.

Depending on the desired finished effect, spread a thin or thick, smooth or textured layer of dimensional paint then embed objects directly into dimensional paint.

For design applications that require a straight edge of dimensional paint, apply low-tack masking tape in desired pattern and spread on dimensional paint. Leave tape in place while embedding objects, taking care not to place objects over tape. After embedding is complete, and while dimensional paint is still wet, carefully remove tape to reveal a straight edge.

Embedding objects after you remove tape can result in pushing the dimensional paint beyond the original tape pattern line. When embedding objects, always let your project dry laying flat on work surface. This will keep embedded objects from slipping while dimensional paint is drying. When applying heavy embedded objects to a permanent vertical surface (such as a wall), use low-tack masking tape to hold the items in place while the dimensional paint dries.

Decorative Tips

Anyone who is familiar with cake decorating will immediately relate to this application. Detail tips (below) can be used to create a variety of shapes when attached to a dimensional paint tube (A). Leaves (B), flowers (C), trims, and dots can be applied directly to the project surface or may be created on waxed paper and adhered to the project surface. Keep in mind that while the dimensional paint may be dry to the touch on the surface, due to the thickness of the dimensional paint in this application, shapes may take longer to completely dry. Be certain to clean detail tips immediately after use with water to remove all dimensional paint; then store for re-use.

Special Effects

Many colors can be created by adding White or Charcoal dimensional paint to solid colors. The Color Chart on pages 120-121 shows different tinting effects, or you may want to mix and match to create your own palettes.

Beautiful marbled effects can be achieved by spreading multiple colors of dimensional paint (D). This technique can be achieved by spreading one color over the surface and then overspreading with complementary or highlight colors. Smooth the colors together with a spreader—just a bit for dramatic marbling—or continue to smear them together for a subtle effect, taking care not to overmix, which can result in a muddy effect.

Metallic Gold dimensional paint used alone creates shimmering, lustrous accents, or you may marbleize any color for an elegant statement.

Antiquing Gel may be added over any dimensional paint project to give an antiqued or aged appearance (E). The Antiquing Gel also enhances the dimensional appearance of the texture in the dimensional paint application. To apply, brush or wipe onto dried dimensional paint and wipe back with lint-free soft cloth. You may also apply the Antiquing Gel to acrylic paint in the same manner.

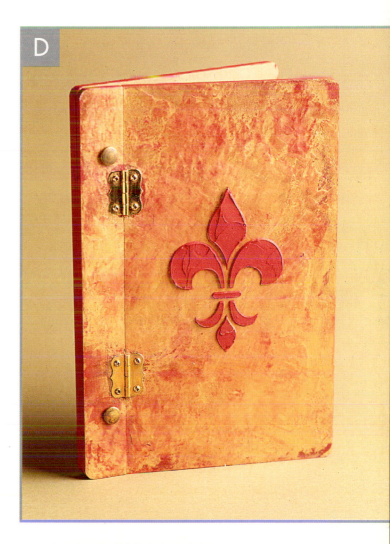

De-Vine Cabinet

Materials

- 1" foam brush
- 1" soft bristle brush
- Acrylic paint—Eucalyptus, Fleshtone Base
- Antiquing gel
- Cabinet
- Dimensional paint—Cashmere
- Dimensional paint spreaders
- Lint-free soft cloth
- Pre-cut stencil—Elegant Vine
- Repositionable stencil adhesive spray
- Varnish—matte

Instructions

1. Apply Fleshtone Base basecoat to wood; let dry.

2. Paint cabinet details with Eucalyptus; let dry.

3. Position stencil. Spread Cashmere dimensional paint over stencil.

4. Carefully lift and clean stencil; let dimensional paint dry.

5. Reposition stencil to complete design; let dimensional paint dry.

6. Apply varnish with bristle brush; let dry.

7. For a light antiquing effect, working small areas at a time, apply antiquing gel with foam brush and immediately wipe off with cloth; let dry.

Project Pointer
Prepping a Wood Cabinet

Whenever working with unfinished wood, it is best to lightly sand the surface in the direction of the grain with fine sandpaper. Use a tack cloth to remove any dust and then apply wood sealer with soft bristle brush.

2 NURTURE MY SOUL

Enjoy projects inspired by colors that are calming and cool and elements that are close to Mother Nature's heart.

Antiquing gel gives this beautiful cabinet its worn, yet sophisticated, look.

Trio of Pots

Materials

- Dimensional paint—Eucalyptus
- Dimensional paint spreaders
- Lint-free soft cloth
- Pre-cut stencil—Elegant Vine
- Repositionable stencil adhesive spray
- Terra-cotta pots

Instructions

1. Clean off any loose dirt or particles on pots with cloth.

2. Position stencil. Spread Eucalyptus dimensional paint over stencil.

3. Carefully lift and clean stencil; let dimensional paint dry.

Project Pointer

Working with Dimensional Paint

To ensure success when using dimensional paint, remember:

- Spray backside of stencil with stencil adhesive spray to keep it firmly attached.

- Begin with small amounts of dimensional paint.

- Be sure dimensional paint dries completely before working in adjacent areas.

- Use plastic zip-top bags to store excess paint during clean up.

When working with terra cotta, be sure the surface is cleaned inside and out.

In the Garden Flower Tin

Materials

³⁄₈" stencil brushes (2)

1" foam brush

No. 2 liner brush

Acrylic paint—Coastline Blue, Sea Grass, Seashell White

Dimensional paint—Almond

Dimensional paint spreaders

Faux-finish glaze base—clear

Metal primer

Palette

Pre-cut stencil—Elegant Vine

Repositionable stencil adhesive spray

Sandpaper—coarse

Sea sponge

Stencil paint crème—Garden Green, Amber

Tin vase

Varnish—matte

Instructions

1. Brush on coat of metal primer on tin with foam brush; let dry.

2. Brush on two coats of Seashell White on bucket and handles; let dry between coats.

3. On palette, mix glaze of one part Sea Grass, two parts glaze base.

4. Use sea sponge to pounce glaze over entire surface; let dry.

5. Position stencil. Spread Almond dimensional paint over stencil.

6. Carefully lift and clean stencil; let dimensional paint dry.

7. Reposition stencil to repeat design; let dry.

8. Reposition stencil. Using stencil brush, stencil leaves randomly with Garden Green.

9. Stencil stem with Amber, shading over into leaves.

10. Brush stripes with Coastline Blue; let dry.

11. Apply varnish; let dry.

Project Pointer

Garden Bench

To create this garden bench, you will also need a crackle medium, Eucalyptus dimensional paint, and a Delicate Vine pre-cut stencil. Apply two Seashell White basecoats to wood; let dry between coats. Position stencil, then spread dimensional paint and let dry. Apply crackle medium according to bottle directions. Overbrush with Seashell White to create crackle effect. After paint dries, lightly sand stenciled areas to reveal dimensional paint.

To achieve a worn look that is ideal for outdoor projects, be sure to use a crackle medium.

Grecian Column

Materials

1" foam brush

1" soft bristle brush

Acrylic paint—Chamomile, Spice Brown

Column

Dimensional paint—Almond

Dimensional paint spreaders

Faux-finish glaze base—clear

Lint-free soft cloth

Pre-cut stencil—Elegant Vine

Repositionable stencil adhesive spray

Instructions

1. Apply Chamomile basecoat; let dry.

2. Position stencil. Spread Almond dimensional paint over stencil.

3. Carefully lift and clean stencil.

4. Move stencil and repeat; let dimensional paint dry.

5. Mix glaze of one part Spice Brown, two parts glaze base.

6. Brush mixed glaze on dried stenciling with foam brush. Gently wipe immediately with cloth to achieve desired antiquing effect.

7. Brush same glaze mix over entire column and gently wipe with cloth; let dry.

Project Pointer
Aging Techniques

Aging a newly painted project can be done in several ways. For the most dramatic effect, apply dimensional paint antiquing gel over your finished project. For a darker antiqued effect, leave most of the gel in the crevices. For a light antiquing, wipe back more of the gel. For other colored antiquing effects, mix faux finish glaze base with any color of acrylic paint. For all antiquing techniques, it is best to work in small areas at a time, applying the gel or glaze with a brush and wiping immediately with a soft lint-free rag.

When working with a large surface such as a column, be sure to reapply stencil adhesive spray as it loses its strength.

Elegant Vine Mirror

Materials

- ½" flat soft bristle brush
- 1" foam brush
- Acrylic paint—Butter Cream, Eucalyptus
- Antiquing gel
- Dimensional paint—Almond
- Dimensional paint spreaders
- Lint-free soft cloth
- Low-tack masking tape
- Mirror with frame
- Pre-cut stencil—Elegant Vine
- Repositionable stencil adhesive spray

Instructions

1. Apply tape over mirror to protect while painting.
2. Apply Butter Cream basecoat; let dry.
3. Apply tape along inner and outer edges.
4. Brush on two coats of Eucalyptus; let dry between coats.
5. Position stencil. Spread Almond dimensional paint over stencil.
6. Carefully lift and clean stencil.
7. Cut leaf cluster from end of stencil and position on mirror.
8. Spread Almond dimensional paint over stencil.
9. Carefully lift and clean stencil; let dimensional paint dry.
10. Using foam brush, brush entire wood surface with antiquing gel. Wipe off excess with cloth.

Before working on a mirror, clean its surface and let it dry completely. That way, paint will adhere without a problem.

Bathroom Set

Materials

- ½" flat soft bristle brush
- Acrylic paint—Butter Cream
- Dimensional paint—Eucalyptus, Sienna
- Dimensional paint spreaders
- Lint-free soft cloth
- Low-tack masking tape
- Pre-cut stencil—Elegant Vine
- Repositionable stencil adhesive spray
- Texture combs
- Wastebasket and tissue holder
- Water

Instructions

1. Apply Butter Cream basecoat; let dry.

2. Tape off diagonal section. Spread Sienna dimensional paint smoothly inside taped area.

3. Comb texture into dimensional paint.

4. Carefully remove tape; let dimensional paint dry.

5. Position stencil. Spread Eucalyptus dimensional paint over stencil.

6. Carefully lift and clean stencil; let dimensional paint dry.

7. Slightly thin Butter Cream with water and dry brush over dimensional paint.

8. Use cloth to remove excess paint until desired effect is achieved.

Project Pointer
Defining Your Style

For a nature bath set, use Spring Green or Green Whisper for a beautiful garden color theme. For a bold country color effect, select Country Red, Bungalow Blue, or Fern Green. If you desire a softer, feminine theme when creating your own Bathroom Set, use Lilac and Almond dimensional paint.

Allow paint to dry completely before moving your stencil to a nearby area on the project.

VASES WITH A VIEW

Materials

Dimensional paint—Cashmere

Dimensional paint spreaders

Glass vases

Low-tack masking tape

Small river rocks, skeleton leaves, cinnamon sticks

Instructions

1. Apply tape to create rectangle.

2. Spread smooth layer of Cashmere dimensional paint.

3. Lay vase flat on work surface.

4. Embed materials into dimensional paint.

5. Remove tape; let dry.

Project Pointer
Stencil Clean-Up

After using dimensional paint, wipe your tools with a paper towel, baby wipe, or damp sponge. Stencils clean easily as long as you don't allow paint to dry on them. To clean, lay stencil on piece of waxed paper and scrape excess off with a spreader. Use damp sponge or wet wipe to clean, front and back. Adhesive can be left on for the next use. Whenever stenciling on glass, it is best to clean the surface with soap and water, rubbing alcohol, or vinegar. Most glass cleaners contain silicone, which can make the glass surface clean but too slick for the dimensional paint to hold firmly.

Inexpensive glass vases can be picked up for a song and easily transformed with dimensional paint.

LEAF IMPRESSIONS

Materials

1" foam brush

Dimensional paint—Green Whisper

Dimensional paint antiquing gel

Dimensional paint spreaders

Fancy yarn

Foam stamp—Aspen Leaf

Lint-free soft cloth

Plaque

Water in small bowl

Instructions

1. Spread generous coat of Green Whisper dimensional paint onto front of plaque; let dry for 10 minutes.

2. Dip foam sponge into water; shake off excess water. Press stamp into dimensional paint and lift.

3. Clean stamp with wet wipe; let dimensional paint dry.

4. Spread generous coat of Green Whisper dimensional paint on sides of plaque; let dry.

5. If desired, brush on antiquing gel.

6. Wipe off excess with cloth; let dry.

7. Tie yarn for hanger.

Project Pointer
Making an Impression

In addition to using foam stamps for making impressions in dimensional paint, you can use found objects from nature. Look for leaves that have strong veins. Press the back of leaf into the dimensional paint for the strongest image. Textured fabric such as burlap also makes an interesting image, as does chicken wire.

Take a walk outdoors and look for interesting leaves sure to leave a lasting impression.

WILD BAMBOO CABINET

Materials

1" foam brush

Acrylic paint—Black Green, Spice Brown

Cabinet

Dimensional paint—Fern Green, Spring Green

Dimensional paint spreaders

Gel stain, medium

Lint-free soft cloth

Low-tack masking tape

Pre-cut background stencil—Bamboo

Repositionable stencil adhesive spray

Instructions

1. Mix gel stain with Spice Brown paint 50:50.

2. Apply mixture to cabinet with foam brush.

3. Let stain soak into wood for one minute. Wipe off excess with cloth; let dry.

4. Tape off areas to be stenciled.

5. Position stencil. Spread Spring Green and Fern Green dimensional paint over stencil.

6. Blend slightly for marbled effect.

7. Carefully lift and clean stencil.

8. Reposition stencil and continue stenciling until desired design is achieved; let dimensional paint dry.

Stencil as much or as little as needed to achieve the desired effect—it's up to you.

Materials

Catchall

1" flat soft bristle brush

3" chip brush

6–drawer box

Acrylic paint—Black Green, Butter Cream

Dimensional paint—Almond, Country Red, Fern Green, Golden Pear

Dimensional paint spreaders

Palette

Paper towels

Pre-cut background stencil—Bamboo

Pre-cut stencil—Floral Border

Repositionable stencil adhesive spray

Sandpaper—fine

Waxed paper

Zip-top bag

Candle

Candle

Dimensional paint—Cashmere, Country Red, Eucalyptus, Golden Pear

Dimensional paint spreaders

Palette

Pre-cut stencil—Pansies

Repositionable stencil adhesive spray

Instructions

Catchall

1. Apply Black Green basecoat to cabinet; let dry.

2. Apply Butter Cream basecoat to drawers; let dry.

3. Spread light coat of Almond dimensional paint to drawer fronts.

4. Lightly drag chip brush horizontally across dimensional paint, then vertically, creating light, dimensional effect similar to burlap; let dimensional paint dry.

   Note: Refer to Wild Bamboo Cabinet (page 36) stencil directions for cabinet top.

Candle

1. On palette, mix Country Red and Golden Pear dimensional paint to create orange.

2. Position stencil. Spread orange dimensional paint over outside petals of floral design.

3. Spread Golden Pear paint over inside of petals and blend two colors together for marbled effect.

4. Spread Eucalyptus dimensional paint over leaf areas.

5. Spread Cashmere over Eucalyptus for marbled effect.

6. Carefully lift and clean stencil.

7. Cut leaf cluster from stencil and position below floral design.

8. Stencil leaves to match prior stenciling.

9. Carefully lift and clean stencil; let dimensional paint dry.

No need to stencil just one item. Adapt a stencil design to a pair of objects for double the impact.

ETHNIC WOODEN BOWL

Materials

1" foam brush

Antiquing gel

Dimensional paint—Almond

Dimensional paint spreaders

Lint-free soft cloth

Pre-cut stencil—Décor Accents

Repositionable stencil adhesive spray

Wooden bowl

Instructions

1. Position stencil. Spread Almond dimensional paint over stencil.

2. Carefully lift and clean stencil.

3. Reposition stencil and apply dimensional paint until pattern effect is achieved; let dimensional paint dry.

4. If antiquing is desired, brush entire wood surface with antiquing gel, working in small sections at a time.

5. Wipe off excess with cloth; let dry.

Project Pointer
Working with a Round Surface

When stenciling on rounded surfaces it is best to select smaller stencil designs or cut your larger stencil into smaller sections. This will make it easier to wrap the stencil design around the rounded surface. Also, depending on how rounded the surface, you may need to secure the edges with low-tack masking tape before stenciling.

3 GLOBAL MOSAIC

A sophisticated richness of earthy colors and
textures defines this worldly style.

While antiquing gel is not necessary for this project, it does lend an aged appearance to the piece.

41

FAUX LEATHER DESK SET

Materials

1" foam brush

1 ½" nylon brush

Acrylic paint—Brown Iron Oxide, Roman Stucco, Rooster Red

Desk set

Dimensional paint—Vintage Leather

Dimensional paint spreaders

Faux-finish glaze base—clear

Palette

Paper towel

Plastic wrap

Pre-cut stencil—Elegant Fleur-De-Lis

Repositionable stencil adhesive spray

Instructions

1. With foam brush, apply two coats of Roman Stucco on all sides; allow to dry completely between coats.

2. To create glaze, mix equal parts Brown Iron Oxide paint and glaze base on palette.

3. Apply glaze mixture to project surface with nylon brush.

4. Immediately dab surface with crumpled plastic wrap. Continue to dab to even out color; let dry.

5. Brush edges and borders with two coats Rooster Red; allow to dry completely between coats.

6. Brush glaze mixture onto Rooster Red. Dab with paper towel to remove excess glaze; let dry.

7. Position stencil. Spread Vintage Leather dimensional paint over stencil.

8. Carefully lift and clean stencil; let dimensional paint dry.

A sophisticated fleur-de-lis stencil design hints at French Country charm.

TUSCAN VILLA WALL TREATMENT

Materials

1" flat soft bristle brush

1" foam brush

Acrylic paint—Brown Velvet, Ivory

Antiquing gel

Dimensional paint—Almond, Country Red, Golden Pear, Sienna, Vintage Leather

Dimensional paint spreaders

Foam stamp—Olive Branch Border

Lint-free soft cloth

Low-tack masking tape

Palette

Pencil

Ruler

Sandpaper—coarse

Satin exterior/interior varnish

Small roller

Tiles (for chair rail)

Varnish—matte

Water in bowl

Wet wipes

Instructions

1. Determine placement of chair rail. Apply tape to wall at desired height.

2. Using paint roller, apply Ivory basecoat to upper half and Brown Velvet basecoat to lower portion.

3. Remove tape; let dry.

4. Spread very heavy coat of Vintage Leather dimensional paint onto lower part of wall; let set about 10 minutes.

5. Dip foam stamp in water; shake off excess. Press foam stamp into dimensional paint.

6. Lift and wipe off stamp with wet wipe, re-dip in water, and stamp again. Repeat until desired pattern is achieved; let dimensional paint dry thoroughly.

7. Place Country Red dimensional paint on palette. Using cloth, pick up small amounts of dimensional paint and rub over entire stamped wall area; let dimensional paint dry.

8. Spread very heavy coat of Almond dimensional paint onto upper part of wall. While this is still wet, go back and apply small amount of Golden Pear and Sienna, spreading to create marbled effect; let dimensional dry.

9. Sand off high points.

10. Brush or roll on varnish on upper portion of wall; let dry.

11. Cover entire surface with antiquing gel using foam brush, working small sections at a time.

12. Wipe off excess with cloth; let dry.

13. For embedded chair rail, apply two strips of tape to create 2" chair rail pattern.

14. Spread generous coat of Sienna dimensional paint between taped areas.

15. Embed tiles into dimensional paint.

16. Brush or roll on final coat of varnish on upper portion of wall.

17. Carefully remove tape; let dimensional paint dry.

Depending on the weight of tiles, it may be necessary to tape over them vertically to hold in place while dimensional paint dries.

MODERN MOSAICS WALL TREATMENT

Materials

¼" low-tack masking or quilter's tape

½" soft bristle brush

2" house painting brush

Acrylic paint—14K Gold, Burnt Sienna, Lichen Grey, Moroccan Red, Pale Gold

Antiquing gel—Black, Brown

Dimensional paint—Charcoal Tint Special Effect, Country Red, Sienna

Dimensional paint spreaders

Foam stamp—Swirl

Lint-free soft cloth

Palette

Paper towels

Pre-cut background stencil—Mosaic Tile

Repositionable stencil adhesive spray

Sandpaper—200 grit

Small bowl of water

Tape measure

Varnish—matte

Wet wipes

Instructions

1. Apply Lichen Grey basecoat; let dry.

2. Mark off tiles into approximately 8 ½" squares using masking tape.

3. Apply Burnt Sienna basecoat to squares.

4. While still wet, blend in some Moroccan Red paint; let dry.

5. Working one square at a time, spread every other square with Sienna dimensional paint.

6. Mix in small amount of Country Red and Charcoal dimensional paint for marbled effect.

7. Dip stamp into water, shake off excess and press into dimensional paint.

8. Lift stamp and clean with wet wipe. Repeat stamping for desired pattern.

9. Carefully lift and remove tape; let dimensional paint dry.

10. For remaining squares, cut stencil to desired size.

11. Position stencil. Spread Sienna, Country Red, and Charcoal over stencil for marbled effect.

12. Lift and clean stencil; let dimensional paint dry.

13. Repeat for each remaining square.

14. Apply varnish with bristle brush; let dry.

15. Mix equal parts Brown and Black antiquing gel and apply with house panting brush over squares.

16. Wipe off excess with cloth, allowing antiquing gel to remain in crevices and cracks; let dry.

17. Dry brush with 14K Gold; let dry.

Charcoal dimensional paint is used to achieve a marbled effect, which provides significant interest to a wall.

SCROLL LINGERIE CHEST

Materials

1" soft bristle brush

Acrylic paint—Cayenne, Roman Stucco

Antiquing gel

Dimensional paint—Cashmere, Country Red

Dimensional paint spreaders

Dresser

Lint-free soft cloth

Low-tack masking tape

Pre-cut stencil—Architectural Elements

Repositionable stencil adhesive spray

Sandpaper—fine, coarse

Scissors

Sealer

Varnish—matte

Wood sealer

Instructions

1. Remove hardware from dresser. If needed, lightly sand with fine sandpaper. If dresser has a finish, remove all loose paint/finish.

2. Brush on coat of sealer; allow to dry before proceeding.

3. Brush on one or two coats of Roman Stucco, adding brush strokes here and there as paint dries. Strokes will later show when antiqued and sanded.

4. Apply Cayenne basecoat to drawer pulls; set aside to dry.

5. Cut stencil to allow for desired placement on drawer. Position stencil on front of drawer, using photo as placement guide.

6. Tape around edges of stencil to help keep dimensional paint from seeping over edges of outside of stencil.

7. Spread Cashmere dimensional paint over stencil.

8. Pick up dab of Country Red and spread over Cashmere to create marbled effect; lift and clean stencil.

9. Repeat to apply dimensional paint designs to entire dresser; allow dimensional paint to dry overnight.

10. Working with small sections at a time, brush antiquing gel over entire chest and drawer fronts, wiping with cloth to remove excess antiquing.

11. When gel has dried, lightly sand all edges of dimensional paint with coarse sandpaper and all flat surfaces with fine sandpaper to reveal brush strokes.

12. Wipe away any sanding dust.

13. Apply two coats of varnish over entire dresser and drawer pulls; allow each coat to dry completely.

14. Reattach hardware.

To ensure that paint takes to its surface, clean piece thoroughly and let dry before beginning project.

FAR EAST DESK SET

Materials

Tray

Dimensional paint—Charcoal Tint Special Effect

Dimensional paint spreaders

Pre-cut stencil—Border Medley

Repositionable stencil adhesive spray

Tray

Varnish—matte

Square Charger

Charger

Dimensional paint—Charcoal Tint Special Effect

Dimensional paint spreaders

Pre-cut stencil—Asian Symbols

Repositionable stencil adhesive spray

Instructions

Tray

1. Position stencil. Spread Charcoal dimensional paint over stencil.

2. Carefully lift and clean stencil; let dimensional paint dry.

3. Apply varnish; let dry.

4. Apply second coat of varnish.

Square Charger

1. Position stencil. Spread Charcoal dimensional paint over stencil.

2. Carefully lift and clean stencil; let dry.

Project Pointer
Creating Zen Appeal

In addition to this Far East Desk Set, a low coffee table would be a beautiful complement to a Zen-themed room. Select furniture pieces with smooth, clean lines and if you can't find just the right height, go ahead and cut the table legs down to your perfect height. To decorate your table, stencil a few rows of bamboo (see Wild Bamboo Cabinet, page 36) along the edges. For a subtle look, select Charcoal Tint Special Effect dimensional paint on a slick black tabletop.

A simple desk set can take on a completely different look by applying a stencil design.

TRAILING VINE

Charger
Materials

- 1" foam brush
- Antiquing gel
- Dimensional paint—Almond
- Dimensional paint spreaders
- Lint-free soft cloth
- Paper towel
- Pre-cut stencil—Climbing Vines
- Repositionable stencil adhesive spray
- Rubbing alcohol
- Wooden charger

Instructions

1. Wipe charger clean with soft cloth.

2. Position stencil. Spread Almond dimensional paint over stencil.

3. Carefully lift and clean stencil.

4. Reposition stencil and apply dimensional paint until surface is covered with desired pattern; let dimensional paint dry.

5. Working small sections at a time, cover entire wood surface with antiquing gel using foam brush.

6. Wipe off excess with cloth; let dry.
   (Note: The same application was used on the lampshade, candles, and clock. The lampshade, however, was not antiqued.)

Project Pointer
Candle Caution

When stenciling and decorating candles with dimensional paint, keep in mind that the candles should be used for decorative uses only. If you wish to light the candles, keep the dimensional paint design at least 3" from the wick and only burn the candles down far enough to insert a tea light candle.

When working with antiquing gel, be sure to remove excess immediately after application.

Ladderback Chair

Materials

- 1" soft bristle brush or small paint roller
- 2" foam brush
- Acrylic paint—Chamomile, Eucalyptus, Spice Brown
- Dimensional paint—Almond
- Dimensional paint spreaders
- Faux-finish glaze base—clear
- Ladderback chair
- Lint-free soft cloth
- Pre-cut stencil—Delicate Vine Border
- Repositionable stencil adhesive spray
- Sandpaper—coarse (optional)
- Small paint roller

Instructions

1. Brush and/or roll on Chamomile basecoat.

2. Apply Eucalyptus basecoat to spindles; let dry.

3. Position stencil. Spread Almond dimensional paint over stencil.

4. Carefully lift and clean stencil; let dimensional paint dry.

5. Mix glaze of one part Spice Brown, two parts glaze base. Apply mixed glaze on dried stenciling with foam brush. Gently wipe with cloth to achieve desired antiquing effect.

6. Brush same glaze mix over entire chair and gently wipe with cloth; let dry.

7. If more worn effect is desired, lightly sand stenciled dimensional paint.

Project Pointer

Keeping Your Furniture Clean

To keep your stenciled furniture clean, simply wipe with a damp sponge or cloth and wipe dry. Keep in mind when applying a stenciled design to the seat of a chair that the chair will likely be used for decorative uses only. Since the design is dimensional, you might find it a bit uncomfortable to sit on the stenciled seat for any length of time.

The key to achieving a distressed, or aged, appearance is to lightly sand paint after it dries.

Materials

Steamer Trunk

1" flat soft bristle brush or small paint roller

1" foam brush

Acrylic paint—Metallic Gold, Spice Brown

Dimensional paint—Cashmere

Dimensional paint antiquing gel

Dimensional paint spreaders

Lint-free soft cloth

Low-tack masking tape

Paper towels

Pre-cut background stencil—Quilted

Repositionable stencil adhesive spray

Trunk

Ochre Wall Treatment

2" house painting brush

Antiquing gel—Brown

Acrylic paint—14K Gold, Pale Gold

Dimensional paint—Almond, Cashmere, Sienna

Dimensional paint spreaders

Lint-free soft cloth

Palette

Paper towels

Sandpaper—200 grit

Varnish—matte

Instructions

Steamer Trunk

1. Tape off all metal areas. Brush or roll on two smooth, even coats of Spice Brown; let dry between coats.

2. Position background stencil. Spread Cashmere dimensional paint over stencil.

3. Carefully remove stencil and clean; let dimensional paint dry.

4. Reposition stencil and repeat to stencil entire trunk; let dry.

5. Cover entire surface with antiquing gel with foam brush, working small sections at a time.

6. Wipe off excess with cloth; let dry.

7. Remove tape. Brush metal areas of trunk with Metallic Gold; let dry.

8. Lightly dry brush over stenciled areas with Metallic Gold; let dry.

Ochre Wall Treatment

1. Spread Cashmere dimensional paint onto wall, adding small amount of Sienna and Almond dimensional paint here and there; let dimensional paint dry.

2. Sand off high peaks. Brush on two coats of varnish; let dry completely between each coat.

3. Brush one even coat of antiquing gel onto surface, working small sections at a time. Wipe off excess with cloth, allowing antiquing gel to remain in crevices and cracks; let dry.

4. Mix equal parts 14K Gold and Pale Gold on palette.

5. Dip brush in paint mixture and brush excess paint onto paper towel.

6. Lightly dry brush over entire surface, allowing paint to adhere to raised areas; let dry.

Metallic Gold can be used alone to create shimmering, lustrous accents, or to marbleize another color for a dramatic statement.

Patchwork Table

Materials

Acrylic paint—Oyster White, Touch O' Pink

Dimensional paint—Almond, Blue Whisper, French Blue, Green Whisper, Lilac, Raspberry, Rose Whisper, Spring Green

Dimensional paint detail tips

Dimensional paint spreaders

Dimensional paint texture combs

Large, soft bristle brush or paint roller

Low-tack masking tape

Pencil

Pre-cut background stencil—Petite Roses

Pre-cut stencil—Vintage Roses

Repositionable stencil adhesive

Ruler

Table

Instructions

1. Brush or roll on two smooth, even coats of Oyster White to entire table.

2. Paint edge of tabletop and shelf, wood plugs on table apron, and bottom trim on apron Touch O' Pink using soft bristle brush.

3. Measure and mark equal sized squares on tabletop (refer to photo).

4. Measure and mark stenciled insert on front of table apron (refer to photo).

5. Measure and mark stenciled portion of shelf (refer to photo).

6. Tape outside marked line on shelf and apron to expose area to be stenciled.

7. Tape as many squares as possible on tabletop.

8. Prepare stencils with adhesive and position Petite Roses stencil over area taped off.

4   FABULOUSLY FEMININE

There's nothing more beautiful than romantic
roses to set a room in bloom.

The more interest you desire, the more important it is to use different texture combs.

Instructions (continued)

9. Spread Rose Whisper dimensional paint over rose areas of stencil and Green Whisper dimensional paint over leaves; clean spreader and pick up tiny bit of Spring Green and spread randomly over leaves and vine to add more color interest.

10. Carefully remove and clean stencil; let dimensional paint dry.

11. Position Vintage Roses stencil on side of table. Stencil with same dimensional paint colors as above.

12. Spread Raspberry dimensional paint to highlight roses and Spring Green dimensional paint to highlight leaves.

13. Carefully remove and clean stencil.

14. Remove tape surrounding stenciled areas as soon as stenciling is complete in that area.

15. Repeat Vintage Roses stencil on opposite side of table; let dimensional paint dry.

16. While waiting for dimensional paint stenciling to dry, start on combed patches of tabletop. Be sure to work in area that does not touch any of wet stenciling.

17. Tape off patch and choose color of dimensional paint to spread into taped area.

18. Using rounded spreader, spread even coat of dimensional paint inside taped area.

19. Comb through dimensional paint to create pattern. Remove tape; let dry thoroughly.

20. When all sections are stenciled and completely dry, add "stitching" lines with small dot detail tip attached to tube of Green Whisper dimensional paint.

21. Practice stitch lines on waxed paper first, then apply along edges of squares and around tabletop; let dimensional paint dry.

Decorative Box Set
Materials
Trinket Box

1" flat soft bristle brush

Acrylic paint—Moss Green

Dimensional paint—Fern Green, Raspberry, Rose Whisper

Dimensional paint detail tips

Dimensional paint spreaders

Palette

Pencil

Pre-cut background stencil—Quilted

Repositionable stencil adhesive spray

Small box

Waxed paper

Large Jewelry Box

1" flat soft bristle brush

Acrylic paint—Peony

Dimensional paint—Fern Green, Green Whisper, Raspberry, Rose Whisper

Dimensional paint spreaders

Pre-cut background stencil—Petite Roses

Repositionable stencil adhesive spray

Small chest

Instructions
Trinket Box

1. Brush two coats of Moss Green on entire box; let dry between coats.

2. Position background stencil on one side of box. Spread Fern Green dimensional paint over stencil.

3. Carefully remove stencil and clean; let dimensional paint dry.

4. Repeat stenciling on each side of box and on box lid; let dimensional paint dry.

5. To create leaves, attach leaf detail tip to Fern Green dimensional paint. Squeeze three large, three medium, and three small leaves on waxed paper; set aside to dry.

6. For rose petals, squeeze small puddle of Raspberry and Rose Whisper dimensional paint onto palette.

7. Draw rose petal shapes on waxed paper.

8. Pick up dimensional paint with pointed spreader and fill in petal pattern, mixing both colors to create highlights on petals; let petals dry thoroughly on waxed paper.

9. When dry, peel leaves and flower petals off waxed paper and arrange on box lid.

10. When satisfied with arrangement, use dab of matching color of dimensional paint to "glue" leaves and petals in place on box lid.

Large Jewelry Box

1. Brush two coats of Peony onto entire box; let dry between coats.

2. Position stencil on one side of box. Spread Raspberry and Rose Whisper dimensional paint over roses on stencil, creating marbled effect.

3. Spread Fern Green and Green Whisper dimensional paint over leaves and vines on stencil, creating marbled effect.

4. Carefully remove stencil and clean; let dimensional paint dry.

5. Repeat stenciling on each side of box.

Most craft and hobby stores stock a wide selection of unpainted boxes ideal for this project.

Wall Treatment

Materials

1" flat soft bristle brush

Acrylic paint—Fleshtone, Peony Pink, Seashell White

Dimensional paint—Cashmere, Green Whisper, Rose Whisper, White

Dimensional paint spreaders

Low-tack masking tape

Paint roller

Palette

Pencil

Pre-cut background stencil—Petite Roses

Pre-cut stencil—Garden Deco Rose

Repositionable stencil adhesive spray

Ruler

Small stones

Tape measure

Instructions

1. Measure for placement of chair rail. Apply tape to wall at desired height.

2. Using paint roller, apply Fleshtone basecoat to bottom half and Seashell White basecoat to upper portion; let dry.

3. Remove tape. Use pencil and ruler to randomly mark 3 ½" squares on upper wall section, allowing two to overlap each other.

4. Brush on two thin basecoats in squares in either Fleshtone or Peony Pink; let dry.

5. Position Garden Deco Rose stencil. Spread White dimensional paint over rose section of stencil; clean spreader.

6. Pick up Cashmere and Rose Whisper dimensional paint on spreader and spread over sections of white to create marbled effect.

7. Spread Green Whisper dimensional paint over leaf sections of stencil; clean spreader.

8. Pick up White dimensional paint on spreader and spread over sections of leaves to create marbled effect.

9. Carefully remove stencil and clean.

10. Repeat stenciling, allowing roses to overlap squares randomly; let dimensional paint dry.

11. For lower wall section, position Petite Roses stencil. Spread White and Cashmere dimensional paint over stencil, lightly smoothing out and blending colors.

12. Carefully lift stencil and clean. Repeat to complete stenciling on lower wall section; let dimensional paint dry.

13. For embedded chair rail, apply two strips of tape to create 2" chair rail pattern.

14. Mix equal parts Cashmere and White dimensional paint on palette. Spread generous coating of mixture between taped areas.

15. Embed stones into dimensional paint. Carefully remove tape; let dry.

By staying within the same color family, you can successfully mix your textures.

FERN GREEN WALL TREATMENT

Materials

Dimensional paint—Fern Green, French Blue, Golden Pear, Green Whisper, Raspberry

Dimensional paint spreaders

Pre-cut stencil—Delicate Vine Border

Repositionable stencil adhesive spray

Instructions

1. Position stencil. Spread Fern Green dimensional paint over leaf portions of stencil; clean spreader.

2. Spread Green Whisper dimensional paint over Fern Green to create marbled effect; clean spreader.

3. Spread Raspberry over flowers, alternating with French Blue.

4. Spread Golden Pear for flower centers.

5. Carefully lift and clean stencil; let dimensional paint dry.

6. Repeat to create desired repeat pattern.

Project Pointer
Perfecting Wall Treatments

Keep in mind when stenciling on a wall that the dimensional paint design will become permanent after it has dried. In order to remove design, you will need to heavily sand the wall. For an interchangeable design, an alternative would be to apply your stenciled design to a wood chair railing. The key to working on a vertical wall surface is to first be certain that you measure correctly to get your design placement straight. Once your wall is marked, carefully place your stencil to align with the placement marks. Stenciling on a vertical wall is easy with dimensional paint because the viscosity, or thickness, of the paint keeps it from dripping.

To ensure that your wall treatment is straight, use a ruler and pencil to draw a straight line to serve as a guide.

ROSE PETAL HEADBOARD BENCH

Materials

Acrylic paint—Mello Yellow, Moss Green, Queen Anne's Lace, Rose Petal Pink

Bench

Ceramic floor tiles

Craft wire—white-coated 26-gauge

Detailing tips

Dimensional paint—White

Dimensional paint detail tips

Dimensional paint spreaders

Flat metal scrapbook words—Create, Dream, Hope, Imagine, Inspire, Believe

Iridescent glass paint

Low-tack masking tape

Masonite board

Pencil

Scissors

Texture combs

Waxed paper

Instructions

Bench Back

1. Screw masonite board onto back of bench.

2. Using pencil, draw pattern lines around spindles.

3. Unscrew board from bench.

4. Tape around pattern lines to create rectangles for design area between spindles.

5. Spread thin coat of White dimensional paint inside taped areas.

6. Comb dimensional paint in wavy pattern.

7. Press floor tiles into combed dimensional paint in random design.

8. Remove tape; let dimensional paint dry.

Invite your guests to hope, dream, and imagine in a bed adorned with this bench-turned-headboard.

Instructions

Flowers, Vines, and Leaves

1. Attach star detail tip to White dimensional paint tube.

2. On waxed paper, practice creating large swirled rose, small and medium star flowers, leaves, and vines. Remember when practicing to scrape off dimensional paint and save it in zip-top bag for use on another project.

3. When ready, create roses and flowers with star detail tip, leaves with leaf tip, and vines with small dot tip on waxed paper, keeping in mind size, shape, and length of vines wanted on finished project; let pieces dry on waxed paper.

4. Select acrylic paint colors and paint pieces; let dry. (We used Rose Petal Pink on the roses, Mello Yellow and Queen Anne's Lace on star flowers, and mixture of half Queen Anne's Lace and Moss Green on leaves and vines.)

5. To create dimensional paint dragonfly, attach small dot detail tip to tube of White dimensional paint.

6. On waxed paper, squeeze two lines to create "X" for wings.

7. Draw line for body and squeeze more dimensional paint for head area.

8. For antennae, cut wire into two 1" lengths, curl ends, and press straight end into head area of dimensional paint; let dry.

9. When dry, remove from waxed paper and paint with iridescent glass paint; let dry.

10. To attach embellishments to design board, dab small amount of White dimensional paint to back of embellishment and glue to board.

11. Continue to glue embellishments until desired finished design is achieved.

12. Use dab of dimensional paint to attach metal words to embellishments. Keep project flat while drying.

13. When completely dry, re-attach design board to back of bench.

Believe

Imagine

Practice creating dimensional flower, leaf, and vine embellishments on waxed paper before applying to finished project.

VINTAGE ROSES BLANKET CHEST

Materials

1" flat soft bristle brush

1" foam brush

Acrylic paint—Light Foliage Green, Medium Foliage Green, Moss Green

Antiquing gel

Chest

Dimensional paint—Almond, Fern Green,

Green Whisper, Raspberry, Rose Whisper

Dimensional paint spreaders

Lint-free soft cloth

Pre-cut stencils—Delicate Vine Border, Flowing Ivy, Vintage Roses

Repositionable stencil adhesive spray

Scissors

Instructions

1. Apply Medium Foliage Green, Light Foliage Green, and Moss Green basecoat to selected areas; let dry.

2. Spread generous coat of Almond dimensional paint in inset areas; let dry.

3. Cut stencils to fit in design areas.

4. Spread Fern Green dimensional paint on leaves; clean spreader.

5. Spread Green Whisper dimensional paint over Fern Green to create marbled effect; clean spreader.

6. Spread Raspberry dimensional paint on roses; clean spreader.

7. Spread Rose Whisper dimensional paint over Raspberry to create marbled effect.

8. Carefully lift and clean stencil; let dimensional paint dry.

9. Working small sections at a time, cover entire surface with antiquing gel using foam brush.

10. Wipe off excess with cloth; let dimensional paint dry.

Everything's coming up roses on this blanket chest, a simple project that transforms an old piece of furniture.

WESTERN ROMANCE FRAME

Materials

1" foam brush

1" soft bristle brush

Acrylic paint—Black, Brown Iron Oxide, Palomino Tan, Rooster Red

Antiquing gel—Black

Brown leather lacing

Clear plastic wrap

Craft foil adhesive

Craft foil sealer

Dimensional paint—any color

Dimensional paint spreader tools

Faux-finish glaze base—clear

Frame with mat

Heat tool with round tip

Lint-free soft cloth

Palette

Pencil

Pre-cut stencil—Architectural Elements

Repositionable stencil adhesive spray

Ruler

Scissors

Silver craft foil

Varnish—matte

Water

Instructions

1. Measure around inside opening of mat board, marking every 1" and ¼" from edge.

2. Using heat tool, burn holes through mat at each mark.

3. Cut large corner design from stencil.

4. Position stencil in one corner of mat. Spread dimensional paint over stencil.

5. Carefully lift and clean stencil. Repeat design in opposite corner.

6. Flip stencil over for remaining two corners; let dimensional paint dry.

7. Apply two coats of Black basecoat to frame; allow to dry between coats.

8. Crumple and straighten out silver foil.

9. Apply foil adhesive, foil, and sealer according to package directions; let dry.

10. Brush antiquing gel over frame. For sponged effect, dab with crumpled plastic wrap; let dry.

11. Apply varnish; let dry.

12. Brush two coats of Palomino Tan onto entire mat board; let dry completely between coats.

13. On palette, create antiquing with 10 percent Rooster Red, 40 percent Brown Iron Oxide, and 50 percent glaze base.

14. Crumple clean plastic wrap and dip into mixture. Dab over entire painted mat board; let dry.

15. Thin Brown Iron Oxide with water to inky consistency.

16. Dip foam brush into mixture. Brush over entire mat. Wipe with cloth to desired antiquing effect; let dry.

17. Apply varnish; let dry.

18. Thread lacing through holes around mat opening.

19. Secure mat and mirror into frame.

5 AMERICAN EXPRESSIONS

Soft and bright red, white, and blue pay tribute to our country's patriotic heritage.

Antiquing gel wiped over this project surface gives the look of gentle aging, updating a once-drab mat.

COUNTRY RED TIN SET

Materials

Oval Container

Dimensional paint—Almond, Country Red

Dimensional paint spreaders

Low-tack masking tape

Oval tin

Pre-cut stencil—Décor Accents

Repositionable stencil adhesive spray

Tin Holders

Dimensional paint—Country Red

Dimensional paint spreaders

Pre-cut stencil—Décor Accents

Repositionable stencil adhesive spray

Square tins

Instructions

Oval Container

1. Position stencil. Spread Almond dimensional paint over stencil.

2. Carefully remove and clean stencil; let dimensional paint dry.

3. Apply tape to create rectangle border, also covering dried stenciled area.

4. Spread Country Red dimensional paint inside tape lines to create large square.

5. Carefully remove tape; let dimensional paint dry.

Tin Holders

1. Position stencil. Spread Country Red dimensional paint over stencil.

2. Carefully remove and clean stencil; let dimensional paint dry.

3. Repeat for each holder.

Project Pointer
Changing Colors

For color variations, mix Country Red and Golden Pear dimensional paint on palette to create a beautiful bright orange. For softer hues of color, add White or Almond dimensional paint and tone down bright colors or darken dimensional paint colors with Charcoal Tint Special Effect.

Use masking tape to be sure paint stays in desired areas. Small sticky notes can also be used in smaller areas.

DENIM BLUE FLORAL FRAME

Materials

1" soft flat bristle brush

Acrylic paint—Chambray Blue, Denim Blue

Dimensional paint—Bungalow Blue

Dimensional paint spreaders

Low-tack masking tape

Pre-cut background stencil—Chintz

Repositionable stencil adhesive spray

Wooden frame

Instructions

1. Apply Chambray Blue basecoat; let dry.

2. Tape front of frame, leaving ½" from edge of frame.

3. Paint edges and ½" from edge of frame with Denim Blue.

4. Remove tape; let dry.

5. Position stencil. Spread Bungalow Blue dimensional paint over stencil.

6. Carefully remove and clean stencil; let dimensional paint dry.

Project Pointer
Just Your Style

This Chintz stencil lends itself to many different tone-on-tone effects. For a very subtle effect, basecoat frame with Magnolia White and Fleshtone acrylic paints and stencil with White dimensional paint. For a feminine flair, basecoat with Peony and Pink Frosting and stencil with Rose Whisper dimensional paint.

Set off a tone-on-tone treatment by using two slightly different hues and watch your photo take center stage.

STACKING COTTAGE BOXES

Materials

Dimensional paint—Blue Whisper, French Blue, Green Whisper

Dimensional paint spreaders

Papier mâché boxes (3)

Pre-cut background stencils—Leaves, Strokework Grid

Pre-cut stencil—Victorian Border

Repositionable stencil adhesive spray

Instructions

Large Box

1. Position bow section of Victorian Border stencil on front of box. Spread Blue Whisper and French Blue dimensional paint over stencil for marbled effect; clean spreader.

2. Position flower garland portion of stencil on top of box and repeat.

3. Carefully lift and clean stencil; let dimensional paint dry.

Medium Box

1. Position Leaves stencil. Spread French Blue dimensional paint over stencil.

2. Carefully lift and clean stencil.

3. Reposition stencil and continue stenciling until desired design is achieved; let dry.

Small Box

1. Cut Strokework Grid stencil to desired size.

2. Position stencil on side of box. Spread Blue Whisper and French Blue dimensional paint over stencil to create marbled effect.

3. Carefully lift and clean stencil. Reposition stencil; continue stenciling until desired design is achieved.

4. Position Victorian Border on top of box. Spread Blue Whisper and French Blue over flower and Green Whisper over leaves.

Mix and match your hues and stencil patterns when working with a series of items that will be displayed together.

Materials

Cabinet

Dimensional paint—White

Dimensional paint spreaders

Pre-cut background stencil—Petite Roses

Repositionable stencil adhesive spray

Sandpaper—coarse

Screen

Instructions

1. Position stencil. Spread White dimensional paint over stencil.

2. Carefully lift and clean stencil; let dry.

3. Sand dried dimensional paint to remove peaks, taking care not to sand screen or cabinet.

4. Repeat stenciling until desired pattern is achieved.

Project Pointer
Stenciling Large Areas

When stenciling a large surface, it is best to trim the end of the stencil so it does not overlap on recently applied dimensional paint. Or, use a hair dryer for a very short time to assist in drying edges where stencil will overlap. A thin layer of dimensional paint typically dries within a half hour; a thick layer could take several hours to dry completely. Remember: If you are stenciling a tabletop in which you plan to place items such as drinking glasses or heavy reading materials, you may want to have a piece of glass cut to fit on top to protect the stenciling.

By gently sanding dimensional paint after it has dried, you will achieve a more finished look.

BUCKET O' FRUIT BASKET

Bucket O' Fruit

Materials

Acrylic paint—Light Ivory

Basket

Dimensional paint—Bungalow Blue, Country Red

Dimensional paint spreaders

Pre-cut stencil—String of Stars

Sandpaper—coarse

Instructions

1. Position stencil along upper edge. Spread Country Red dimensional paint over stencil; let dry.

2. Carefully lift and clean stencil; let dimensional paint dry.

3. Reposition to repeat design.

4. Position stencil on side of basket.

5. Spread Bungalow Blue dimensional paint over large star sections of stencil.

6. Carefully lift and clean stencil; let dimensional paint dry.

7. Reposition to repeat design; let dimensional paint dry.

8. Dry brush entire basket with acrylic paint.

9. Carefully sand stenciled dimensional paint areas, allowing color of dimensional paint to show.

Project Pointer
Basket Makeovers

A variety of baskets in many shapes and sizes can be found at most yard sales or thrift stores. This is a quick and easy project that adds design character and flair and gives plain baskets new life. Keep in mind that with this worn stenciling technique, you can overpaint with any acrylic color. For best results, select dimensional paint and acrylic over colors that are contrasting.

Layer paint and gently sand to reveal a hint of the base color, thus giving the project a worn appearance.

FLORAL MOSAIC FLOWER TIN

Materials

Dimensional paint—White

Dimensional paint spreaders

Found objects—glass pieces, plain and print glass mosaic tiles

Low-tack masking tape

Tin vase

Instructions

1. Determine size and shape of embedding area. Apply tape to surface.

2. Determine pattern of embedding items by laying out on work surface first. Spread generous smooth coat of White dimensional paint to embedding area.

3. Lay tin down on work surface. Secure to keep tin from rolling.

4. Embed items into dimensional paint.

5. Carefully remove tape. Keep tin on side while drying.

Project Pointer
No Grout Required

For anyone who has tried traditional mosaic projects, you'll love this quick and easy technique that requires no grouting. Simply use the dimensional paint as "glue" to hold your tile and glass pieces in place. For best results, measure and lay out your pattern on paper first, then apply your dimensional paint and transfer the embedded items one by one onto your surface.

Just about any found items can be embedded in dimensional paint to create an interesting objet d'art.

FLORAL MOSAIC TIN BAG

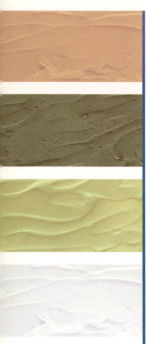

Materials

Dimensional paint—Cashmere, Eucalyptus, Green Whisper, White

Dimensional paint spreaders

Glass mosaic pieces

Palette

Pre-cut stencil—Rose and Lilacs

Sandpaper—medium

Tin bag

Instructions

1. Position stencil. Spread White dimensional paint over rose portion of stencil.

2. On palette, mix Green Whisper, Eucalyptus, and Cashmere dimensional paint together with spreader. Spread mixture onto leaf portion of stencil.

3. Carefully lift and clean stencil; let dimensional paint dry.

4. Sand or file edges of glass mosaic pieces to remove sharp edges.

5. Lay tin down on work surface. Spread White dimensional paint on back of tiles and press in place on tin and around edge of stenciled design.

6. Keep tin on side while drying.

Project Pointer
Breaking China Pieces

Vintage reproduction tiles can easily be found at your local craft store. For more traditional mosaic, scour your local thrift stores, yard sales, and flea markets for chipped china that can be broken into pieces suitable for mosaic projects. When breaking china, be sure to wear protective goggles. Place the piece in a hand towel then hit it with a hammer, breaking until desired sizes are achieved.

This bag is not for shopping! It can serve as a catchall or to hold plants indoors or out.

Picnic Basket

Materials

Dimensional paint—Almond, Bungalow Blue, Country Red, French Blue, White

Dimensional paint spreaders

Palette

Picnic basket

Pre-cut background stencil—Stars, Stripes

Repositionable stencil adhesive spray

Instructions

1. On palette, mix three parts White dimensional paint, one part Almond dimensional paint.

2. Position Stars stencil. Spread mixture over stencil.

3. Carefully remove and clean stencil; let dimensional paint dry.

4. Position Stars stencil over handle. Spread mixture over stencil; repeat on other handle.

5. Carefully remove and clean stencil; let dimensional paint dry.

6. Position Stripes stencil. Spread each stripe with different color of dimensional paint, alternating Bungalow Blue, Country Red, and French Blue; let dimensional paint dry.

Project Pointer
Selecting the Right Stencil

With the wide selection of stencil designs available, you can embellish your picnic basket or design your party décor to achieve one of a variety of themes or looks. For a retro effect, select fruit motifs in a worn stenciling effect; for a beach picnic, consider a seascape or nautical theme.

A traditional red, white, and blue color palette give patriotic flair to this picnic basket.

Candle and Hurricane

Materials

Candle

Candle

Dimensional paint—Bungalow Blue, Country Red, French Blue

Dimensional paint spreaders

Low-tack masking tape—various widths

Paper towel

Rubbing alcohol

Hurricane

Dimensional paint—Almond, White

Dimensional paint spreaders

Hurricane

Palette

Pre-cut background stencil—String of Stars

Repositionable stencil adhesive spray

Instructions

Candle

1. Wipe candle with rubbing alcohol to remove residue.

2. Tape off stripes of varying widths on candle.

3. Position stencil. Spread Bungalow Blue, Country Red, and French Blue dimensional paint to create stripes.

4. Carefully lift tape; let dimensional paint dry.

Hurricane

1. On palette, mix one part White, one part Almond dimensional paint.

2. Position stencil. Spread mixture over stencil.

3. Carefully lift and clean stencil; let dimensional paint dry.

Project Pointer
Keeping Glass Clean

To keep your glass surface clean after stenciling, wipe with a damp cloth and wipe to dry. When the dimensional paint is dry, it is very durable, but cleaning compounds could discolor the paint and prolonged exposure to water can affect the strength of the bonding to the glass.

When working with candles, clean surface with rubbing alcohol before you begin stenciling.

Materials

1" soft bristle brush

Acrylic paint—Light Ivory, Rooster Red

Dimensional paint—Country Red, Golden Pear

Dimensional paint spreaders

Furniture

Pre-cut stencil—Leaves and Berries

Repositionable stencil adhesive spray

Sandpaper—coarse

Instructions

1. Brush on Rooster Red basecoat to selected areas of kitchen furniture; let dry.

2. Position stencil. Spread Country Red and Golden Pear dimensional paint over stencil using marbling technique.

3. Carefully lift and clean stencil.

4. Reposition to repeat design; let dimensional paint dry.

5. Overbrush stenciled design and remaining unpainted wood with Light Ivory; let dry.

6. Carefully sand paint off stenciled dimensional paint areas, allowing color of dimensional paint to show.

Mixing deep, saturated hues are ideal for blending and marbling furniture projects.

ROOSTER RED TRAY

Materials

1" soft bristle brush

Acrylic paint—Opaque Red, Pigskin

Crackle medium

Dimensional paint—Country Red, Golden Pear

Dimensional paint detail tips

Dimensional paint spreaders

Pre-cut stencil—American Farm

Repositionable stencil adhesive

Tray

Instructions

1. Brush on Opaque Red basecoat; let dry.

2. Crackle with Pigskin over basecoat on floor of tray; let dry.

3. Position stencil on tray. Spread Country Red dimensional paint over rooster and hen bodies and Golden Pear over legs and feet; let dry.

4. Attach small dot detail tip to tube of Golden Pear dimensional paint.

5. Create tiny Golden Pear dimensional paint dots on tray with detail tip; let dimensional paint dry.

Project Pointer
Using Paint Detail Tips

When taking a break from a project, cover paint detail tips with their protective caps so paint doesn't dry out. When finished with tip, remove from paint tube and use cleaning tool or pipe cleaner to clean out excess paint. Rinse tips with warm water immediately, before paint dries in tip. Or, put tip in cup of warm water and clean later.

The small dot paint detail tip makes creating polka dots a cinch. Be sure to clean tips right after use.

CHERRIES JUBILEE LAMP, BULLETIN BOARD & CABINET

Materials

1" flat soft bristle brush

Acrylic paint—Bungalow Blue, Coastline Blue

Dimensional paint—Country Red, Fern Green, White

Dimensional paint detail tips

Dimensional paint spreaders

Lamp, bulletin board, cabinet

Low-tack masking tape

Pre-cut stencil—Beautiful Fruits

Repositionable stencil adhesive

Scissors

Waxed paper

Instructions

Lampshade

1. Paint trim of lampshade with Bungalow Blue using flat brush; let dry.

2. Cut cherries from stencil to make it easier to stencil on curved surface.

3. Position stencil on shade. If needed, tape sides of stencil to shade.

4. Spread Country Red dimensional paint over cherries on stencil and Fern Green dimensional paint over leaves and stems.

5. Carefully remove and clean stencil.

6. Reposition stencil and continue stenciling cherries on lampshade as desired; let dimensional paint dry.

Bulletin Board

1. Brush on Coastline Blue basecoat over cork.

2. Brush on Bungalow Blue basecoat over frame; let dry.

3. Position stencil in corners of cork. Spread Country Red dimensional paint over cherries on stencil and Fern Green dimensional paint over leaves and stems.

4. Attach large dot detail tip to tube of White dimensional paint. Practice your dots on piece of waxed paper first, then apply dots in random pattern on bulletin board; let dimensional paint dry.

Cabinet

1. Brush on Coastline Blue basecoat to cabinet doors; let dry.

2. To create color variation on cabinet top and sides, brush Bungalow Blue and Coastline Blue with flat brush in a "slip-slap" motion; let dry.

3. Position stencil. Spread dimensional paint over stencil.

4. Attach large dot detail tip to tube of White dimensional paint. Practice dots on piece of waxed paper first, then apply dots in random pattern on front of cabinet; let dimensional paint dry.

Fresh, bright red cherries will brighten any little girl's room, especially when used on different projects.

MOSAIC FRUIT BREADBOX & PLAQUES

Materials

1/4" red grosgrain ribbon

1/2" flat soft bristle brush

Acrylic paint—Magnolia White, Old Parchment, Tomato Spice

Breadbox and plaques (4)

Dimensional paint—Country Red, Fern Green, Golden Pear, Lilac, Spring Green

Dimensional paint spreader tools

Low-tack masking tape

Palette

Pre-cut stencil—Mosaic Fruit

Repositionable stencil adhesive spray

Sandpaper—coarse

Scissors

Sea sponge, small

Water

Instructions

Breadbox

1. Position stencil on front of breadbox. Secure edges with tape.

2. Spread Country Red dimensional paint over apples, cherries, and border.

3. Spread Golden Pear over pear.

4. Spread Fern Green over leaves and stems.

5. Carefully remove and clean stencil.

6. Reposition stencil to create fruit designs and border on sides; let dimensional paint dry.

7. Pour Old Parchment and Magnolia White onto palette. Wet sea sponge and wring out water.

8. Dip sponge into both colors and pounce over entire surface of breadbox; let dry.

9. Carefully sand paint off fruit and border, allowing color of dimensional paint to show.

Tiles

1. Apply Old Parchment basecoat on plaques.

2. Pounce over basecoat with dampened sea sponge dipped in Magnolia White.

3. Paint edges of plaques with Tomato Spice.

4. Cut stencil to create a separate stencil for each fruit.

5. Position apple stencil on plaque. Spread Spring Green dimensional paint over leaves; wipe spreader clean.

6. Dip end of spreader into small amount of Golden Pear and spread along edges of leaves, blending colors together.

7. Spread Country Red over apple; wipe spreader clean. Then spread Golden Pear in upper right-hand corner. Lightly blend colors to create highlight.

8. Remove and clean stencil; let dimensional paint dry.

9. Create Cherry plaque following same directions.

10. Position grapes stencil on plaque. Spread Lilac dimensional paint over grapes; wipe spreader clean. Then spread Golden Pear on right side, blending colors together.

11. Spread Spring Green over leaves. Highlight with Golden Pear.

12. Remove and clean stencil; let dimensional paint dry.

13. Position Pear stencil on plaque. Spread Golden Pear dimensional paint over pear; wipe spreader clean.

14. Dip end of spreader into Country Red and spread over base and side of pear, blending colors together.

Create different themes with the same paint method by simply changing the stencils for each project.

MELLO YELLOW CANISTERS & PEAR WALL

Materials

Canisters

1" soft bristle brush

Acrylic paint—Magnolia White, Mello Yellow, Vintage Leather

Canisters—metal

Dimensional paint—Golden Pear

Dimensional paint spreader tools

Metal primer

Pre-cut stencils—Beautiful Fruits, 2" Upper & Lower Case Calligraphy, Calligraphy Alphabet

Repositionable stencil adhesive spray

Sandpaper—medium, coarse

Pear Wall

1" soft bristle brush or small roller

Acrylic paint—Magnolia White

Dimensional paint—Golden Pear

Dimensional paint spreader tools

Pre-cut stencil—Beautiful Fruits

Repositionable stencil adhesive spray

Sandpaper—coarse

Instructions

Canisters

1. Sand canisters to remove any rust and to give "tooth" to surface.

2. Brush on one coat of primer; let dry.

3. Position pear stencil. Spread Golden Pear dimensional paint over stencil.

4. Carefully lift and clean stencil; let dimensional paint dry.

5. Overbrush stenciled design with Mello Yellow; let dry.

6. Carefully sand paint off stenciled design, allowing color of dimensional paint to show.

7. Stencil lettering with Vintage Leather; let dry.

Pear Wall

1. Position stencil. Spread Golden Pear dimensional paint over stencil.

2. Carefully lift and clean stencil; let dimensional paint dry.

3. Overbrush stenciled design with Magnolia White.

4. Carefully sand paint off stenciled design, allowing color of dimensional paint to show.

Fruit stencils are ideal choices for kitchen projects. You can even stencil the wall to continue the theme.

RETRO LAMPSHADE & NIGHTSTAND

Materials

1" soft bristle brush

Acrylic paint—Blue Lagoon, Fuchsia, Magnolia White, Spring Green

Dimensional paint—White

Dimensional paint spreader tools

Lampshade and nightstand

Low-tack masking tape

Pre-cut stencil—Daisies

Repositionable stencil adhesive spray

Instructions

Lampshade

1. Paint lampshade two coats of Fuchsia; let dry between coats, and thoroughly after final coat.

2. Position stencil on shade; secure edges with tape. Spread White dimensional paint over stencil.

3. Carefully remove and clean stencil.

4. Reposition stencil and continue stenciling until desired design is achieved; let dimensional paint dry.

Nightstand

1. Apply 2-3 coats of Magnolia White to frame or cabinet part of table; let dry between coats, and thoroughly after final coat.

2. Apply 2-3 coats of Blue Lagoon, Fuchsia, or Spring Green to each drawer; let dry between coats, and thoroughly after final coat.

3. Position stencil on drawer front. Spread White dimensional paint over stencil.

4. Carefully remove and clean stencil.

5. Reposition stencil and continue stenciling until desired design is achieved; let dimensional paint dry.

When stenciling on a curved surface, secure edges of stencil with low-tack masking tape to hold in place.

MOSAIC HEART

Materials

Craft knife

Craft wire—black-coated 26-gauge

Dimensional paint—Bungalow Blue, Cashmere, Charcoal Tint, Country Red, Fern Green, Golden Pear, Vintage Leather

Dimensional paint detail tips

Dimensional paint spreaders

Found objects—flat-backed marbles, mirror tiles, mosaic tiles, poetry beads

Frame with removable glass

Low-tack masking tape

Pencil

Scissors

Waxed paper

Instructions

1. Remove glass from frame. Cover entire glass surface with strips of tape.

2. Draw heart design on tape. Use craft knife to cut along pattern line.

3. Remove tape from inside pattern line. You have just created your own tape stencil.

4. Spread Cashmere dimensional paint inside tape lines.

5. Embed beads, mosaic tiles, and found objects into dimensional paint.

6. Carefully remove tape; let dimensional paint dry.

7. To create dimensional paint butterfly, attach small dot detail tip to tube of Bungalow Blue dimensional paint. On waxed paper, squeeze two lines to create "X" for base of wings. Continue to draw around "X" to widen wings using photograph as guide; remove tip and clean.

8. Attach tip to tube of Fern Green dimensional paint. Continue to draw with paint to create butterfly wings; remove tip and clean.

9. Attach tip to Vintage Leather dimensional paint. Draw line for body and squeeze more dimensional paint for head.

10. For antennae, cut wire into two $\frac{1}{2}$" lengths, curl ends, and press straight end into head area of dimensional paint; let dry.

11. When dry, remove from waxed paper. Apply dab of dimensional paint to back of butterfly and glue to frame.

12. To create remaining frame embellishments, first use small dot detail tip with Fern Green to draw looping vine. Next, use leaf detail tip with Fern Green to create leaves on vine. Use star tip for flowers in Country Red, Golden Pear, and Bungalow Blue. Use small dot detail tip for berries in Country Red. Keep in mind that you might want to practice designs on waxed paper first.

13. Create ladybugs with large and small dot detail tips in Country Red and Charcoal Tint dimensional paint and black wire for antennae.

Now that you have the tools, it's time to make a gift to bestow on someone special.

inspire

believe

dream

When using paint detail tips, be sure to clean thoroughly before changing dimensional paint color.

Materials

1" soft bristle brush

Acrylic paint—Metallic Gold, Sandstone, colors of your choice

Adhesive-backed fabric

Canvas

Decoupage medium

Dimensional paint—Almond, Blue Whisper, Eucalyptus, Rose Whisper, White

Dimensional paint spreaders

Found objects—beads, mosaic tiles

Handmade papers

Paper paint—gold

Pre-cut background stencils—2" Lower Case Calligraphy, Scroll, Butterflies and More, Décor Accents, Magnolia, Strokework Grid

Repositionable stencil adhesive spray

Scrapbook papers

Instructions

1. Apply Sandstone basecoat to canvas; let dry.

2. Brush adhesive-backed fabric with Metallic Gold; let dry.

3. Lay scrapbook and handmade papers on canvas. Move elements around until you achieve desired layout. Keep in mind that some areas will be filled in with stenciling and texturing.

4. Brush decoupage medium onto back of papers and glue to canvas; let dry.

5. Remove grid backing from fabric and adhere to canvas.

6. Lay stencils on canvas. Move around until you achieve desired layout.

7. Stencil with acrylic paint in some parts of canvas and stencil with dimensional paint in other areas.

8. Use dimensional paint embedding techniques, combing, and texturing to create your own masterful collage!

You don't need an art degree to create these one-of-a-kind canvases. Choose alternate hues to match particular colors in a room.

EUCALYPTUS CANDLE

Materials

Candle

Dimensional paint—Eucalyptus

Dimensional paint detail tips

Dimensional paint spreaders

Low-tack masking tape

Painted wood medallion

Paper towel

Rubbing alcohol

Waxed paper

Instructions

1. Clean surface of candle with rubbing alcohol; let dry.

2. Position tape to mask off area you wish to embellish.

3. Spread generous coat of Eucalyptus dimensional paint on candle inside taped area.

4. Press medallion into dimensional paint.

5. Carefully remove tape; let dimensional paint dry.

6. Attach large dot detail tip to tube of Eucalyptus dimensional paint.

7. Practice dots on waxed paper first, then apply dots along edge; let dimensional paint dry.

Project Pointer
Straighten Up

When creating straight lines with dimensional paint, simply apply low-tack masking tape in desired pattern. Be certain to firmly press along the edge to create a tight bond that will prevent dimensional paint from seeping under the tape. Spread dimensional paint to desired texture, then immediately remove tape. When you carefully remove the tape, the result is a crisp line.

Avoid using dimensional paint on the top of your candle if you plan to light the candle.

TRIPLE DIAMOND CANDLE

Materials

Candle

Dimensional paint—Cashmere, Vintage Leather

Dimensional paint spreaders

Gold-finish thumbtacks

Paper towel

Pre-cut background stencil—Harlequin

Repositionable stencil adhesive spray

Rubbing alcohol

Instructions

1. Clean surface of candle with rubbing alcohol; let dry.

2. Position stencil. Spread Cashmere and Vintage Leather dimensional paint over stencil, mixing to create marbled effect.

3. Carefully remove and clean stencil; let dimensional paint dry.

4. Press thumbtacks into candle.

Project Pointer
Choosing Your Embellishments

There are a variety of beautiful embellishments you can embed into dimensional paint. For a beach theme, select small shells; for a Zen candle, select metal poetry words; for a fabulously feminine look, pearls, rhinestones, or beads are pretty choices; and for contemporary style, flat-backed iridescent marbles are a great choice.

Thumbtacks are quick and easy embellishments that turn a plain candle into a showpiece.

COLLAGE FRAME & TRINKET BOX

Materials

1/8" stencil brush (2)

1/4" stencil brush (2)

1/2" soft bristle brush

1" foam brush

Acrylic paint—Apple Green, Boston Fern, Persimmon, Tuscan Red, Western Sunset Yellow

Antiquing gel—Brown

Beaded trim

Craft box with lid

Craft glue

Dimensional paint—White

Dimensional paint spreaders

Frame

Lint-free soft cloth

Pre-cut background stencil—Flowing Roses, Petite Roses

Repositionable stencil adhesive spray

Varnish—matte

Instructions

1. Position Petite Roses stencil. Spread White dimensional paint over stencil on side of box.

2. Carefully remove and clean stencil. Reposition to repeat stencil; let paint dry.

3. Using foam brush, brush Western Sunset Yellow over entire box; let dry.

4. Place small puddle of Boston Fern on palette. Using bristle brush, thin paint with water to an inky consistency and brush on stripes on lid in one direction; let dry.

5. Brush stripes in opposite direction to create plaid background; let dry.

6. Reposition Petite Roses stencil over dried dimensional paint. Using 1/4" stencil brush, lightly color roses with Persimmon.

7. Shade with 1/8" stencil brush using Tuscan Red.

8. Use second 1/4" stencil brush to color leaves with Apple Green and shade with 1/8" brush using Boston Fern. Repeat this coloring technique on entire stenciled surface; let dry.

9. Cut desired pattern from Flowing Roses stencil. Position on frame. Spread dimensional paint over stencil.

10. Carefully remove and clean stencil; let dimensional paint dry.

11. Reposition Flowing Roses stencil over dried dimensional paint and color with stencil brushes as described above; let dry. Repeat for lid of trinket box.

12. Brush antiquing gel on entire surface.

13. Immediately wipe back with cloth for soft antiquing effect; let dry.

14. Apply varnish; let dry.

15. Glue beaded trim in place; let dry.

Just about any frame with a flat surface can be used for this project. Consider a small matching box for bedside trinkets.

ROSE WHISPER SCRAPBOOK COVER

Materials

¼" stencil brush

1" soft bristle brush

Acrylic paint—Butter Cream, Fleshtone Base, Raw Linen, Seashell White

Craft glue

Dimensional paint—Almond, Green Whisper, Rose Whisper

Dimensional paint spreaders

Lace trims, buttons, ribbons

Low-tack masking tape

Palette

Paper towel

Pre-cut stencil—2" Upper & Lower Case Calligraphy, Deco Roses

Pre-cut background stencil—Petite Roses

Repositionable stencil adhesive spray

Scrapbook

Instructions

1. Disassemble scrapbook. Apply Seashell White basecoat to front cover, Fleshtone Base basecoat to spine, and Raw Linen basecoat to back.

2. Tape off squares on front cover. Using photo as guide, paint five color blocks from color palette selections by taping off two unattached blocks at a time; remove tape.

3. When dry, re-tape next sections and paint.

4. Remove tape and repeat to complete; let dry.

5. Position Deco Rose stencil. Spread Almond dimensional paint over stencil; clean spreader.

6. Spread small amount of Rose Whisper dimensional paint over rose area, blending for marbled effect; clean spreader.

7. Spread small amount of Green Whisper dimensional paint over leaf areas, blending for marbled effect.

8. Carefully lift and clean stencil; let dimensional paint dry.

9. Tape around color block where you plan to position Petite Roses background stencil. This will help keep dimensional paint from being stenciled into another section.

10. Position stencil. Spread Almond dimensional paint over stencil, blending with Rose Whisper and Green Whisper dimensional paint to complement Deco Rose stencil.

11. Carefully lift and clean stencil; let dimensional paint dry.

12. Position Calligraphy stencil letter over Raw Linen color block. Pour small puddle of Butter Cream on palette.

13. Dip stencil brush into paint and brush excess paint onto paper towel.

14. When applying paint with stencil brush, use very little paint in dry-brush technique. (You might want to practice this brushing technique on piece of scrap paper before stenciling on album.)

15. Use soft, circular motion to apply light coat of Butter Cream over Calligraphy stencil.

16. Carefully lift and clean stencil.

17. Glue embellishments onto remaining color blocks.

Create a scrapbook cover just as special as the memories it holds. Just about any scrapbook can be transformed.

Materials

- Aluminum foil
- Craft glue
- Dimensional paint—Almond, Rose Whisper, White
- Dimensional paint detail tips
- Dimensional paint spreaders
- Iron and hard ironing surface
- Iron-on stitch effect transfers—Lazy Daisies
- Palette
- Repositionable stencil adhesive spray
- Serrated knife
- Straight pins or T-pins
- Toothpicks
- Waxed paper
- White florist wire—26-gauge or white chenille stem (for bow)
- White foam (1) 12" x 18" x 1", (2) 6" x 12" x 1", (1) 3" x 6" x 2"
- White sheer and satin ribbons—¼", ½", and 1"

Instructions

1. Cut 12" x 18" piece of foam in half to make two 12" x 9" sections.

2. Dip ends of toothpicks into glue and press into top of one piece of foam.

3. Stack pieces on top of each other, securing with toothpicks.

4. Cut 3" off end of 6" x 12" pieces of foam to form 6" x 9" pieces.

5. Dip ends of toothpicks into glue and press into top of one piece of foam.

6. Stack pieces on top of each other, securing with toothpicks.

7. Using spreader tool, on palette mix following tubes of dimensional paint colors to make "frosting": (1 tube) Rose Whisper; (3 tubes) White; (½ tube) Almond.

8. Using spreader tool, apply "frosting" to sides and top of bottom layer. Use broad spreader to smooth.

9. Repeat for each layer of cake.

10. Set each layer aside on piece of waxed paper to dry separately.

11. Cut daisy iron-on transfer into three equal sections.

12. Lay ribbon on foil. Using photo as guide, determine placement of each daisy border section and iron onto ribbon.

13. Beginning with bottom layer, refer to photo to lay out ribbon in plaid pattern.

14. Secure ends of ribbon with straight pins to bottom of this layer, or so they will be hidden by next layer.

15. Repeat for middle and top layers. For best effect, be certain ribbons match up from one layer to next.

16. To create scalloped effect along edge of ribbon, attach small dot detail tip to tube of White dimensional paint.

17. Practice scallop technique on piece of waxed paper first. Then embellish 1"-wide ribbons with scalloped edge of dimensional paint; set aside to dry thoroughly.

18. To assemble, dip ends of toothpicks into glue. Place toothpicks into underside of middle layer.

If you can frost a cake, you can create this dazzling centerpiece perfect for special occasions such as a baby shower or birthday.

	WHITE	ALMOND	CASHMERE	SIENNA
TEXTURE MAGIC COLOR				
MARBLED WITH ANOTHER COLOR	*Cashmere*	*Eucalyptus*	*Sienna*	*Vintage Leather*
MARBLED WITH CHARCOAL				
MARBLED WITH WHITE	*n/a*			
TINTED WITH CHARCOAL				
TINTED WITH WHITE	*n/a*			
MARBLED WITH METALLIC GOLD				
PURE COLOR WITH ANTIQUING GEL OVER TOP				

	GOLDEN PEAR	COUNTRY RED	RASPBERRY	ROSE WHISPER
TEXTURE MAGIC COLOR				
MARBLED WITH ANOTHER COLOR	*Sienna*	*Almond*	*Pink Whisper*	*Almond*
MARBLED WITH CHARCOAL				
MARBLED WITH WHITE				
TINTED WITH CHARCOAL				
TINTED WITH WHITE				
MARBLED WITH METALLIC GOLD				
PURE COLOR WITH ANTIQUING GEL OVER TOP				

VINTAGE LEATHER	EUCALYPTUS	FERN GREEN	SPRING GREEN	GREEN WHISPER
Cashmere	*Sienna*	*Spring Green*	*Almond*	*Fern Green*

BUNGALOW BLUE	FRENCH BLUE	BLUE WHISPER	DEEP LILAC	LILAC
Blue Whisper	*Bungalow Blue*	*Almond*	*Lilac*	*Almond*

Color swatches may print differently than actual paint.

121

Tiffany Windsor

Tiffany Windsor has mastered the art of creative living. Born into an artistic, entrepreneurial family, she found success expressing her talents in many different arenas early in life. Tiffany, daughter of Aleene Jackson, inventor of Aleene's Tacky Glue, grew up transforming everyday objects into artistic creations, bejeweling cigar boxes and designing chenille treasures to her heart's content. As an author, storeowner, and television producer, Tiffany has been sharing inspiring ideas for the home and heart for more than a decade. She hosted Aleene's Creative Living on The Nashville Network and Craft, Home and Style on The Hallmark Channel, authored several books, and launched numerous online women's magazines. Tiffany wrote and hosted her first prime-time special, The Magic of Christmas, which aired on TNN in 1998. The one-hour program featured exquisite holiday decorations, celebrity interviews, and cooking and last-minute crafting ideas for the holidays. In 2003, Tiffany joined Delta Technical Coatings as Director of Consumer Inspiration, focusing her creative energies on inspiring and educating consumers on the fun of crafting and creative expression through her online magazine, www.homespirations.com.

Metric Equivalency Charts

inches to millimeters and centimeters							yards to meters									
inches	mm	cm	inches	cm	inches	cm	yards	meters	yards	meters	yards	meters	yards	meters	yards	meters
⅛	3	0.3	9	22.9	30	76.2	⅛	0.11	2⅛	1.94	4⅛	3.77	6⅛	5.60	8⅛	7.43
¼	6	0.6	10	25.4	31	78.7	⅛	0.11	2⅛	1.94	4⅛	3.77	6⅛	5.60	8⅛	7.43
½	13	1.3	12	30.5	33	83.8	¼	0.23	2¼	2.06	4¼	3.89	6¼	5.72	8¼	7.54
⅝	16	1.6	13	33.0	34	86.4	⅜	0.34	2⅜	2.17	4⅜	4.00	6⅜	5.83	8⅜	7.66
¾	19	1.9	14	35.6	35	88.9	⅝	0.46	2½	2.29	4½	4.11	6½	5.94	8½	7.77
⅞	22	2.2	15	38.1	36	91.4	⅝	0.57	2⅝	2.40	4⅝	4.23	6⅝	6.06	8⅝	7.89
1	25	2.5	16	40.6	37	94.0	¾	0.69	2¾	2.51	4¾	4.34	6¾	6.17	8¾	8.00
1¼	32	3.2	17	43.2	38	96.5	⅞	0.80	2⅞	2.63	4⅞	4.46	6⅞	6.29	8⅞	8.12
1½	38	3.8	18	45.7	39	99.1	1	0.91	3	2.74	5	4.57	7	6.40	9	8.23
1¾	44	4.4	19	48.3	40	101.6	1¼	1.03	3¼	2.86	5⅛	4.69	7¼	6.52	9⅛	8.34
2	51	5.1	20	50.8	41	104.1	1¼	1.14	3¼	2.97	5¼	4.80	7¼	6.63	9¼	8.46
2½	64	6.4	21	53.3	42	106.7	1⅜	1.26	3⅜	3.09	5⅜	4.91	7⅜	6.74	9⅜	8.57
3	76	7.6	22	55.9	43	109.2	1½	1.37	3½	3.20	5½	5.03	7½	6.86	9½	8.69
3½	89	8.9	23	58.4	44	111.8	1⅝	1.49	3⅝	3.31	5⅝	5.14	7⅝	6.97	9⅝	8.80
4	102	10.2	24	61.0	45	114.3	1¾	1.60	3¾	3.43	5¾	5.26	7¾	7.09	9¾	8.92
4½	114	11.4	25	63.5	46	116.8	1⅞	1.71	3⅞	3.54	5⅞	5.37	7⅞	7.20	9⅞	9.03
5	127	12.7	26	66.0	47	119.4	2	1.83	4	3.66	6	5.49	8	7.32	10	9.14
6	152	15.2	27	68.6	48	121.9										
7	178	17.8	28	71.1	49	124.5										
8	203	20.3	29	73.7	50	127.0										

INDEX

Page 20

De-Vine Cabinet

Delta Ceramcoat Acrylic Paint

• Eucalyptus 28 006

• Fleshtone Base 2082

Delta Ceramcoat Interior Spray Varnish—Matte 07 203 0045

Delta Repositionable Stencil Adhesive Spray 28 169 0028

Delta Stencil Magic Stencil

• Elegant Vine 95 667 0018

Delta Texture Magic Dimensional Paint

• Cashmere 28 003

Delta Texture Magic Easy-Grip Spreaders 28 100 0028

Delta Texture Magic Special Effects Antiquing Gel 28 021 0202

Page 22

De-Vine Trio of Pots

Delta Stencil Magic Pre-Cut Stencil

• Elegant Vine 95 667 0018

Delta Texture Magic Dimensional Paint

• Eucalyptus 28 006

Delta Texture Magic Easy-Grip Spreaders 28 100 0028

Page 24

In the Garden Bench Bench

Delta Ceramcoat Acrylic Paint

• Seashell White 2541

Delta Ceramcoat Crackle Medium 07 009 0200

Delta Repositionable Stencil Adhesive Spray 28 169 0028

Delta Stencil Magic Stencil

• Delicate Vine Border 95 662 0018

Delta Texture Magic Dimensional Paint

• Eucalyptus 28 006

Delta Texture Magic Easy-Grip Spreaders 28 100 0028

Flower Tin

Delta Ceramcoat Acrylic Paint

• Coastline Blue 2574

• Sea Grass 2549

• Seashell White 2541

Delta Ceramcoat Metal Primer 07 010 0202

Page 26

Grecian Column

Delta Ceramcoat Acrylic Paint

• Chamomile 2567

• Spice Brown 2049

Delta Repositionable Stencil Adhesive Spray 28 169 0028

Delta Stencil Magic Stencil

• Elegant Vine 95 667 0018

Delta Texture Magic Dimensional Paint

• Almond 28002

Delta Texture Magic Easy-Grip Spreaders 28 100 0028

Page 28

Elegant Vine Mirror

Delta Ceramcoat Acrylic Paint

• Butter Cream 2523

• Eucalyptus 28 006

Delta Repositionable Stencil Adhesive Spray 28 169 0028

Delta Stencil Magic Pre-Cut Stencil

• Elegant Vine 95 667 0018

Delta Texture Magic Dimensional Paint

• Almond 28 002

Delta Texture Magic Easy-Grip Spreaders 28 100 0028

Page 30

Trailing Vine Bathroom Set

Delta Ceramcoat Acrylic Paint

• Butter Cream 2523

Delta Repositionable Stencil Adhesive Spray 28 169 0028

Delta Stencil Magic Stencil

• Elegant Vine 95 667 0018

Delta Texture Magic Dimensional Paint

• Eucalyptus 28 006

• Sienna 28 004

Delta Texture Magic Easy-Grip Spreaders 28 100 0028

Delta Texture Magic Easy-Grip Texture Combs 28 101

Page 32

Vases with a View

Delta Texture Magic Dimensional Paint

• Cashmere 28 003

Delta Texture Magic Easy-Grip Spreaders 28 100 0028

Page 34

Leaf Impressions

Delta Decorative Foam Stamp

• Aspen Leaf 72019

Delta Texture Magic Dimensional Paint

• Green Whisper

Delta Texture Magic Easy-Grip Spreaders 28 100 0028

Delta Texture Magic Special Effects Antiquing Gel 28 021 0202

Page 36

Wild Bamboo Cabinet

Delta Ceramcoat Acrylic Paint

• Black Green 2116

• Spice Brown 2049

Delta Repositionable Stencil Adhesive Spray 28 169 0028

Delta Stencil Magic One-Step Background Stencil

• Bamboo 95 871 1013

Delta Texture Magic Dimensional Paint

• Fern Green 28 007

• Spring Green 28 008

Delta Texture Magic Easy-Grip Spreaders 28 100 0028

Page 38

Pansies Perfected Catchall & Candle Catchall

Delta Ceramcoat Acrylic Paint

• Black Green 21116

• Butter Cream 2523

Delta Repositionable Stencil Adhesive Spray 28 169 0028

Delta Stencil Magic Floral Border 95 354 0012

Delta Stencil Magic One-Step Background Stencil

• Bamboo 95 871 1013

Delta Texture Magic Dimensional Paint

• Almond 28 002

• Fern Green 28 007

• Golden Pear 28 010

• Country Red 28 011

Delta Texture Magic Easy-Grip Spreaders 28 100 0028

Candle

Delta Repositionable Stencil Adhesive Spray 28 169 0028

Delta Stencil Mania Stencil

• Pansies 97 037 0710

Delta Texture Magic Dimensional Paint

• Cashmere 28 003

• Country Red 28 011

• Eucalyptus 28 006

• Golden Pear 28 010

Delta Texture Magic Easy-Grip Spreaders 28 100 0028

Page 40

Ethnic Wooden Bowl

Delta Repositionable Stencil Adhesive Spray 28 169 0028

Delta Stencil Mania Stencil

• Décor Accents 97 061 0710

Delta Texture Magic Dimensional Paint

• Almond 28 002

Delta Texture Magic Easy-Grip Spreaders 28 100 0028

Delta Texture Magic Special Effects Antiquing Gel 28021

Page 42

Faux Leather Desk Set

Delta Ceramcoat Acrylic Paint

• Brown Iron Oxide 2023

• Roman Stucco 2581

• Rooster Red 2578

Delta Ceramcoat Faux Glaze Base— Clear 55 401 0800

Delta Repositionable Stencil Adhesive Spray 28 169 0028

Delta Stencil Magic Stencil

• Elegant Fleur De Lis 95 671 0018

Delta Texture Magic Dimensional Paint

• Vintage Leather 28 005

Delta Texture Magic Easy-Grip Spreaders 28 100 0028

Page 44
Tuscan Villa Wall Treatment

Delta Ceramcoat Acrylic Paint

• Brown Velvet 2109
• Ivory 2306

Delta Decorative Foam Stamp

• Olive Branch Border 74009

Delta Satin Exterior/Interior Varnish 7003

Delta Texture Magic Dimensional Paint

• Almond 28 002
• Country Red 28001
• Golden Pear 28012
• Sienna 28004
• Vintage Leather 28005

Delta Texture Magic Easy-Grip Spreaders 28 100 0028

Delta Texture Magic Special Effects Antiquing Gel 28021

Page 46
Modern Mosaics Wall Treatment

Delta Ceramcoat Acrylic Paint

• 14K Gold 2604
• Burnt Sienna 2032
• Cashmere 28 003
• Lichen Grey 2118
• Moroccan Red 2552
• Pale Gold 2624

Delta Ceramcoat Black Antiquing Gel 7302

Delta Ceramcoat Brown Antiquing Gel 7301

Delta Ceramcoat Matte Varnish 7008

Delta Decorative Foam Stamp—Swirl 72047

Delta Repositionable Stencil Adhesive Spray 28 169 0028

Delta Stencil Magic One-Step Background Stencil

• Mosaic Tile 95 869 1013

Delta Texture Magic Dimensional

Paint

• Charcoal Tint Special Effect 28 020
• Country Red 28 011
• Sienna 28 004

Delta Texture Magic Easy-Grip Spreaders 28 100 0028

Page 48
Scroll Lingerie Chest

Delta Ceramcoat Acrylic Paint

• Cayenne 2428
• Roman Stucco 2581

Delta Ceramcoat Interior Spray Varnish—Matte 07 203 0110

Delta Repositionable Stencil Adhesive Spray 28 169 0028

Delta Stencil Magic Stencils

• Architectural Elements 95 676 00518

Delta Texture Magic Dimensional Paint

• Cashmere 28 003
• Country Red 28 011

Delta Texture Magic Easy-Grip Spreaders 28 100 0028

Delta Texture Magic Special Effects Antiquing Gel 28 021 0202

Page 50
Far East Desk Set

Delta Repositionable Stencil Adhesive Spray 28 169 0028

Delta Stencil Mania Stencil

• Asian Symbols 97 035 0710
• Border Medley 95 304 0012

Delta Texture Magic Dimensional Paint

• Charcoal Tint Special Effect 28 020

Delta Texture Magic Easy-Grip Spreaders 28 100 0028

Page 52
Trailing Vine Charger

Delta Repositionable Stencil Adhesive Spray 28 169 0028

Delta Stencil Mania Stencil

• Climbing Vines 97 062 0710

Delta Texture Magic Dimensional Paint

• Almond 28 002

Delta Texture Magic Easy-Grip Spreaders 28 100 0028

Delta Texture Magic Special Effect Antiquing Gel 28021

Page 54
Trailing Vine Ladderback Chair

Delta Ceramcoat Acrylic Paint

• Chamomile 2567
• Eucalyptus 28 006
• Spice Brown 2049

Delta Ceramcoat Faux Finish Glaze Base—Clear 55 401 0800

Delta Repositionable Stencil Adhesive Spray 28 169 0028

Delta Stencil Magic Stencil

• Delicate Vine Border 95 662 0018

Delta Texture Magic Dimensional Paint

• Almond 28 002

Page 56
Steamer Trunk & Ochre Wall Treatment

Delta Ceramcoat Acrylic Paint

• Metallic Gold 2600
• Spice Brown 2049

Delta Ceramcoat Antiquing Gel

• Brown 7301

Delta Repositionable Stencil Adhesive Spray 28 169 0028

Delta Satin Exterior/Interior Varnish 7003

Delta Stencil Magic One-Step Background Stencil

• Quilted 95 863 1013

Delta Texture Magic Dimensional Paint

• Almond 28 002
• Cashmere 28 003
• Sienna 28004

Delta Texture Magic Easy-Grip Spreaders 28 100 0028

Delta Texture Magic Special Effects Antiquing Gel 28 021 0202

Page 58
Whispering Roses Patchwork Table

Delta Ceramcoat Acrylic Paint

• Oyster White 2492
• Touch O' Pink 3565

Delta Repositionable Stencil Adhesive Spray 28 169 0028

Delta Stencil Magic One-Step Background Stencil

• Petite Roses 95 858 1013

Delta Stencil Magic Stencil

• Vintage Roses 95 666 0018

Delta Texture Magic Dimensional Paint

• Almond 28 002
• Blue Whisper 28 016
• French Blue 28 015
• Green Whisper 28 009
• Lilac 28 018
• Raspberry 28 012
• Rose Whisper 28 013
• Spring Green 28 008

Delta Texture Magic Easy-Grip Spreaders 28 100 0028

Delta Texture Magic Easy-Grip Texture Combs 28 101

Delta Texture Magic Easy-Twist Detail Tips 28 102 0028

Page 62
Whispering Roses Box Set

Trinket Box

Delta Ceramcoat Acrylic Paint

• Moss Green 2570

Delta Repositionable Stencil Adhesive Spray 28 169 0028

Delta Stencil Magic One-Step Background Stencil

• Quilted 95 863 1013

Delta Texture Magic Dimensional Paint

• Fern Green 28 007
• Raspberry 28 012
• Rose Whisper 28 013

Delta Texture Magic Easy-Grip Spreaders 28 100 0028

Delta Texture Magic Easy-Twist Detail Tips 28 102 0028

Large Jewelry Box

Delta Ceramcoat Acrylic Paint

• Peony 2579

Delta Repositionable Stencil Adhesive

Spray 28 169 0028

Delta Stencil Magic One-Step Background Stencil

• Petite Roses 95 858 1013

Delta Texture Magic Dimensional Paint

• Fern Green 28 007
• Green Whisper 28 009
• Raspberry 28 012
• Rose Whisper 28 013

Delta Texture Magic Easy-Grip Spreaders 28 100 0028

Whispering Roses Wall Treatment

Delta Ceramcoat Acrylic Paint

• Fleshtone 2019
• Peony Pink 2579
• Seashell White 2541

Delta Repositionable Stencil Adhesive Spray 28 169 0028

Delta Stencil Magic One-Step Background Stencil

• Petite Roses 95 858 1013

Delta Stencil Magic Stencil

• Garden Deco Rose 95 673 0018

Delta Texture Magic Dimensional Paint

• Cashmere 28 003
• Green Whisper 28 009
• Rose Whisper 28 013
• White 28 001

Delta Texture Magic Easy-Grip Spreaders 28 100 0028

Fern Green Wall Treatment

Delta Repositionable Stencil Adhesive Spray 28 169 0028

Delta Stencil Magic Stencil

• Delicate Vine Border 95 662 0018

Delta Texture Magic Dimensional Paint

• Fern Green 28 007
• French Blue 28 015
• Golden Pear 28 010
• Green Whisper 28 009
• Raspberry 28 012

Delta Texture Magic Easy-Grip Spreaders 28 100 0028

Rose Petal Headboard Bench

Delta Ceramcoat Acrylic Paint

• Mello Yellow 2553
• Moss Green 2570
• Queen Anne's Lace 2017
• Rose Petal Pink 2521

Delta Texture Magic Dimensional Paint

• White 28001

Delta Texture Magic Easy-Grip Spreaders 28100

Delta Texture Magic Easy-Grip Texture Combs 28101

Delta Texture Magic Easy-Twist Detailing Tips 28102

Vintage Roses Blanket Chest

Delta Ceramcoat Acrylic Paint

• Light Foliage Green 2537
• Medium Foliage Green 2536
• Moss Green 2570

Delta Repositionable Stencil Adhesive Spray 28 169 0028

Delta Stencil Magic Stencil

• Delicate Vine Border 95 662 0018
• Flowing Ivy 95 244 0018
• Vintage Roses 95 666 0018

Delta Texture Magic Dimensional Paint

• Almond 28 002
• Fern Green 28 007
• Green Whisper 28 009
• Raspberry 28 012
• Rose Whisper 28 013

Delta Texture Magic Easy-Grip Spreaders 28 100 0028

Delta Texture Magic Special Effects Antiquing Gel 28 021 0202

Western Romance Frame

Delta Ceramcoat Acrylic Paint

• Black 2506

• Brown Iron Oxide 2023
• Palomino Tan 2108
• Rooster Red 2578

Delta Ceramcoat Antiquing Gel— Black 07 302 0202

Delta Ceramcoat Exterior/Interior Varnish—Matte 07 040 0202

Delta Ceramcoat Faux Finish Glaze Base—Clear 55 401 0202

Delta Renaissance Foil Silver Leafing Kit 06 920 0056

Delta Repositionable Stencil Adhesive Spray 28 169 0028

Delta Stencil Magic Stencil

• Architectural Elements 95 676 0018

Delta Texture Magic Dimensional Paint (color of choice)

Delta Texture Magic Easy-Grip Spreaders 28 100 0028

Country Red Tin Set

Oval Container

Delta Repositionable Stencil Adhesive Spray 28 169 0028

Delta Stencil Magic Stencil

• Décor Accents 97 061 0710

Delta Texture Magic Dimensional Paint

• Almond 28 002
• Country Red 28 011

Delta Texture Magic Easy-Grip Spreaders 28 100 0028

Tin Holders

Delta Repositionable Stencil Adhesive Spray 28 169 0028

Delta Stencil Mania Stencil

• Décor Accents 97 061 0710

Delta Texture Magic Dimensional Paint

• Country Red 28 011

Delta Texture Magic Easy-Grip Spreaders 28 100 0028

Denim Blue Floral Frame

Delta Ceramcoat Acrylic Paint

• Chambray Blue 2514
• Denim Blue 2477

Delta Repositionable Stencil Adhesive Spray 28 169 0028

Delta Stencil Mania Stencil

• Chintz 95 861 1013

Delta Texture Magic Dimensional Paint

• Bungalow Blue 28 014

Delta Texture Magic Easy-Grip Spreaders 28 100 0028

Stacking Cottage Boxes

Delta Repositionable Stencil Adhesive Spray 28 169 0028

Delta Stencil Magic One-Step Background Stencil

• Leaves 95 857 1013
• Strokework Grid 95 868 1013

Delta Stencil Magic Stencil

• Victorian Border

Delta Texture Magic Dimensional Paint

• Blue Whisper 28 016
• French Blue 28 015
• Green Whisper 28 009

Delta Texture Magic Easy-Grip Spreaders 28 100 0028

White-on-White Photo Screen & Cabinet

Delta Repositionable Stencil Adhesive Spray 28 169 0028

Delta Stencil Magic One-Step Background Stencil

• Petite Roses 95 858 1013

Delta Texture Magic Dimensional Paint

• White 28 001

Delta Texture Magic Easy-Grip Spreaders 28 100 0028

Bucket O' Fruit Basket

Delta Repositionable Stencil Adhesive Spray 28 169 0028

Delta Stencil Magic Stencil

• String of Stars 95 113 0012

Delta Texture Magic Dimensional